MEGURIAI

Nobuko's American Journey

Faith Nobuko Araki Barcus

authorHOUSE®

AuthorHouse™
1663 Liberty Drive
Bloomington, IN 47403
www.authorhouse.com
Phone: 1-800-839-8640

First published by AuthorHouse   3/15/2010

ISBN: 978-1-4490-4701-6 (sc)
ISBN: 978-1-4490-4702-3 (hc)

Library of Congress Control Number: 2009911823

Printed in the United States of America
Bloomington, Indiana

This book is printed on acid-free paper.

MEGURIAI (meh-guri-ai): NOBUKO'S AMERICAN JOURNEY is a chronicle of happenings in my life as I lived in two countries, Japan and the United States, through war and peace. The seed of my interest in America was planted from my father's book on his student day experiences from 1918 to 1921 when he came to America on a government scholarship. "Meguriai" in Japanese means "chance meeting." We meet thousands of people throughout our lives, and some of these encounters leave a life-long impact on our lives. That is how I met Earle on December, 1945, at the US-Japan combined Messiah chorus planned to encourage peace and friendship between the two nations. Earle was in the base section and me in the alto section. We fell in love, were married for 56 years, and had a daughter and two sons.

My mother kept all my letters, and after her death in 1955, my sisters returned them to me. Similarly, I saved all the letters of my parents and sisters that crossed the Ocean. These letters were a precious source of information on happenings that took place in my life during the past half century. Also over 50 photo albums I meticulously created helped to bring to life distant memories of the past.

I would like to thank Ms. Misao Kaneko for her computer expertise in helping me navigate the unfamiliar world. Inclusion of the photos and other images would not have been possible without her help.

To Earle

CONTENTS

INTRODUCTION

Nobuko's American Journey is a chronicle of my life journey through two very different cultures, East and West. For more than five decades, I have struggled to bring together the best of both, to make my own culture and to find my own identity as a woman, wife, mother, and Japanese American.

In 1995, the United States celebrated the fiftieth anniversary of the end of the Pacific War with numerous parades and recognition of war heroes and stories of heroic battles fought in the Pacific. Veteran pilots told of *the bomb* to end all wars, of how it was dropped on Hiroshima and, three days later, on Nagasaki—the bomb that instantaneously burnt to a crisp untold number of mostly women, children, and elderly people and left radiation in the atmosphere to take many more lives in the following years.

But there was never a mention of the civilian casualties suffered in the firebombing of cities in Japan. Before 1995, I never talked about my wartime experience with any Americans, not even my husband or children. I was following the Japanese custom of *"Kusai Mono Niwa Futa O Shiro,"* meaning, if something smells bad, keep a lid on—don't talk about unpleasant things. But I felt compelled to let people know that a war is not just about the heroics of soldiers. That year, I broke my silence and wrote about my wartime experience in the Tokyo bombing when I was a teenager. I felt the real victims were innocent civilians who had no say in the politics of war yet were the ones who lost their homes, loved ones, and even their own lives without glory or honor.

The article was featured in the *Boston Sunday Globe* on July 30, 1995. The reaction was overwhelming. Friends, and even people I'd never met, called and wrote me of their shock to learn that there were firebombings of Tokyo, Osaka, and other major cities of Japan before the atom bombs were dropped on Hiroshima and Nagasaki. They thanked me for sharing a piece of history that they didn't know.

I sent a copy of the article to a dear friend of thirty years in Virginia. She did not respond for several months. I wondered why. Later she confessed that the revelation of my wartime experience in the article put her "into identity crises" because she knew nothing about my other life in Japan. She went through a dilemma of asking, *Just who is Nobuko Barcus anyway?* and thanked me for finally opening up and sharing my story with others. Hers and others' reactions to my article planted a seed in my mind that I had a story to tell.

When I semiretired from my full-time work, I set out to put in chronological order my letters, photos, and diaries from the time I left Japan in 1948 to today. Fortunately, I had saved all the letters from my parents, sisters, and friends. When my mother died, my sister sent me back the letters I had written to my mother so that I had a written dialogue between my mother and me spanning the six years up to her death. My sister also sent me the diary my mother kept during her trip to America in 1952. My father's books helped me reconstruct the distant past. They were *Dream Journey*, which chronicles my father's student days in America, published in 1922; *Around the World in 33 Days,* about my father's race around the world in 1928, published in 1929; and *History of Efficiency Management, Parts I and II*, the case studies of my father's consulting work from 1922 to 1970, published in 1954 and updated in 1971. My father's biography, written by Seiki Ikai and titled *Gohri No Nekki Kyu* (*Hot Air Balloon of Efficiency*), was published by Yonkai Shobo Publishing Company in Tokyo in 1991.

Going through the old letters and diaries was an amazing experience for me, at once exhilarating and sometimes painful. Many totally forgotten incidents came to life again. I laughed and wept along the way. I translated my father's books, *Dream Journey* and *Around the World in*

33 Days. People's reactions to the translations, especially to *Around the World in 33 days*, were a range of amazement and curiosity and desire to know more. This led me to writing my memoir, an undertaking to help me understand my destiny in America. I hope readers will gain deeper understanding of two very diverse cultures.

CHAPTER I: THE PACIFIC WAR

"What a Stupid Thing Japan Got Herself Into!"

On December 7, 1941, when I was fourteen years old, I was listening to a weekly radio show (decades before TV) when the program stopped suddenly.

The shaking voice of an announcer came over the radio. "One moment, please. An important announcement is to follow."

Moments later, the announcer continued: "Japan has bombed Pearl Harbor in Hawaii! Japan has entered into a war with the United States!"

We could almost feel the announcer's shaking body as he repeated this incredulous news over and over again. We waited impatiently, trying to understand what this meant to our lives.

A few days later, we received a postcard from our father, who was away on business. In his characteristically bold and flamboyant writing, he said:

Misses Keiko, Nobuko and Aiko,

What a stupid thing Japan got herself into! Japan will lose. Be forewarned.

Father

In later years, such postcards would never have passed the government censor. I was a high school student and hadn't the vaguest idea what a war would mean to our daily lives. My sisters and I went to school as usual, did our homework, and practiced our piano. I continued to attend my ballet classes three times a week. But from the serious looks on adults' faces wherever we went and the way they intently gathered around the radio, I sensed that something horrible was going to happen in our lives.

My father had been actively involved in promoting the industrial development of Japan since 1933, when he was elected to head a think tank, Kokka Keizai Kenkyujo (National Economy Research Institute), to come up with a national plan to make Japan into a global economic power. In 1940, he was working as a management consultant for Kawasaki, the largest aircraft company in Japan at that time. He writes in his memoir that, from the kind of production that was going on at the company, he sensed that Japan was getting ready for a war. He felt that the country was totally unprepared for such an event, and if Japan were to engage in a war, she would need to streamline her economic planning. So he went to see General Tojo, the supreme commander, and presented his plan. After thirty minutes of talk, Tojo said, "We have no plans to go to war."

A year later, in the spring of 1941, my father was more and more convinced that with General Tojo now as the prime minister, the current administration was heading for a war with the United States. He again visited Tojo and told him that he knew from his years living in America that the United States was a sleeping giant and her power could not be underestimated; Tojo would be a traitor to Japan if he started a war that was doomed to fail. But this time my father was only given a five-minute meeting and was told that, even if Japan were to enter into a war, the Japanese possessed a special divine spirit that would lead the country to victory.

My father continued to speak out against the war at the Rotary Club and other public gatherings, much to the dismay of his family, friends, and office staff, who feared that some might question his allegiance to his country and harm him.

Ever since he had seen the devastation of World War I during his travel through Europe in 1921, my father had been a strong proponent for peace. Also, he was against the war because he loved his country and foresaw Japan's defeat.

Repressive Government

In 1943, the war still seemed remote to us; except for rationing of food and scarcity of certain luxuries it had little effect on our day-to-day lives. I was still in high school and was taking ballet lessons. One day, a military policeman came knocking on the door at our ballet school. With a fierce grimace, he shouted, "Do you realize we are in time of war? What kind of citizens are you to be engaging in such a decadent activity as ballet and listening to foreign music! You should be ashamed of yourselves!"

Unpatriotic to study ballet...

Our teacher, who had the premier ballet company in Japan at that time, tried to explain that the ballet had actually originated in Russia and that the music we danced to was by Russian or Polish composers and not by Americans, to no avail. The military police barked at us aspiring ballerinas, who were trembling with fear and clustered around our teacher, "Engaging in such a foreign activity as ballet with foreign music is tantamount to being a traitor to the Japanese spirit!"

After that, we practiced with the windows closed even on the hottest days so that the music of Chopin and Tchaikovsky, which was neither American nor English, would not be heard. As the war intensified and we no longer heard much victorious news, such repressive acts by the military government increased.

In the spring of 1944, I was a college freshman studying English at Tsuda Juku University, the sister college of Bryn Maur College, with a vague dream of going to study in America some day as my father had done. In 1940s Japan, a girl going to college was not as common as it is today, and most colleges were gender divided. It would be many decades before Tokyo University, the Harvard of Japan, and other prestigious universities such as Keio and Waseda would open their doors to women.

At school, we were warned not to open English books on the train or bus for fear that some people might get upset that we were studying the enemy language. True, we were at war with the very country of my dreams, but with youthful naiveté and optimism, I thought my dream would come true someday, somehow.

Firebombing of Tokyo

Sporadic air raids on Tokyo began in 1944, mostly on major train stations and airfields. I had to go through Shinjuku, a major train station, to get to my college. Worried about my safety, my mother put me in the dormitory.

HISTORY

Burned into memory

A survivor of the Tokyo firebombing recalls life among the ruins of war

BY FAITH NORIKO BARCUS

In the American mind, the final chapter of World War II is defined by the bombings of Hiroshima and Nagasaki. But as the 50th anniversary of those epic events approaches, others remember an earlier horrendous chapter in the war against Japan: the firebombing of its cities by the Allies in spring 1945. Indeed, more people were killed by the firebomb inferno that swept across Tokyo on the night of March 9-10 than were killed on Aug. 6 at Hiroshima.

It is that part of the war — when huge fires leveled neighborhoods and cities, asphyxiating or burning alive thousands of Japanese families — that Faith Noriko Barcus remembers. Now a resident of Jerusalem Plaza, she was an 18-year-old college student living with her family in Tokyo when wave after wave of low-flying US planes began dropping incendiary bombs on the Japanese mainland. She remembers trying to live a normal life amid haunting scenes of devastation and death.

> I know Japan is going to lose the war. We may all die in the bombing. I'm going to give you a choice. You may go to our summer home in the country where life is relatively safer, or you may stay in Tokyo and die with your family.

In 1945, US B-29s dropped thousands of firebombs on Tokyo, taking many thousands of lives and leaving the city in charred rubble.

5

One Sunday, I was walking along the cabbage fields after a weekend visit with my family, laden with some hard-to-get food in my backpack. The wailing air-raid siren rang out, and a few minutes later, I heard the familiar rumbling drone of the B-29's. I could see the specks in the sky growing larger and larger. P-51 fighter planes were escorting the bombers on the way to do damage to the Tachikawa Air Base, which was near my college. In my naive young mind, the bombs would fall where the bomber intended. Since I was several miles away from the air base, I thought I would be safe. Besides, I was just a harmless young woman who carried no weapon of destruction. Who would want to harm me? So, I kept walking. Suddenly one of the escorting planes descended low enough for me to make out a figure inside the cockpit. He began to shoot at me. Rat-a-tat-tat! I jumped in a vegetable patch holding my head, prostrate. My face touched the ground, and I could smell the earth. I held my breath.

For an instant, the friendly smiling faces of Americans I had seen in the yellowed photos of my father's student days in Ohio flashed through my mind. All the stories of kind Americans who had helped my father and my dream of going to America just like he had done simply didn't square in my mind with them shooting at me. Maybe the pilot didn't mean to kill anyone but just wanted to scare us. The plane flew away. I heard in the distance the sound of the bombs falling and the ground antiaircraft guns responding. I ran to my dormitory as fast as my legs could carry me.

You May Die Tomorrow

Toward the end of 1944, the defeat of Japan in the Pacific War seemed imminent, and the air-raid bombing of Japan's major cities became more frequent. One day, my father called for a family conference. By the tone of his voice, we sensed that he was going to talk about something very important, and we looked to him with heightened anticipation. He told us solemnly, "We may all die from the bombing. You may go to our summer home in the mountains where life will be relatively safer, or you can stay in the city and take a chance. You have your choice."

We sat stunned for a moment.

My mother said firmly, "My place is here with my family," looking at my father and my pregnant sister whose husband was at war.

Kiku, who had been with the family as our maid, nanny, and surrogate mother for more than twenty years, and who had lost her parents some years back, said, "This is *my* family. I'll stay here."

"I, too, will stay in Tokyo," I declared. "I'll not give up my education!"

My sister, Aiko, who was in eighth grade, the sweet and agreeable baby of the family, was silent for a long time. Then, she blurted out, "I'm going to our country home. I am too young to die!" Her words and countenance, filled with determination, took everyone's breath away.

After much discussion about the Spartan life she would have to live in the country alone and the need for her to adjust to a country school with unfamiliar customs, Aiko's resoluteness won over my father's reluctance.

Aiko left Tokyo to live alone at our summer home in the village of Oiwake at the foot of Mount Asama. With the help of a nearby farmer who was the caretaker of our house, she learned how to do her own cooking, cleaning, and washing. It is a wonder that she did not suffer from malnutrition as she mostly subsisted on potatoes and noodles. She later told me that she did not bathe very often because filling the tub with a hand pump was too taxing for a fifteen-year-old girl who was quite small in stature. She would just go to our caretaker's house for a bath. She commuted to a country school on the train, clad in farmer-style trousers, blouse, and geta (wooden flip-flops). Most of all, she learned the joys and struggles of being independent.

Food Shortage, School Factory, and Power Cutback

My dormitory life was austere since everything was rationed. The school did the best it could, but I remember being hungry often. There was a small charcoal burner at the end of the corridor on each floor. My dorm-mate and I would go to a farm nearby and buy some sweet potatoes and roast them over the charcoal fire to stave off our hunger.

During 1944, when bombs destroyed many of the munitions factories in Tokyo, our college gymnasium was converted into a munitions factory. All students after class were required to work as factory workers. I remember standing in line, my head tightly covered with a bandana, filing nuts and bolts for hours on end. Our studies and factory work were often disrupted by air raids. As soon as the ear piercing air-raid siren rang out, we would drop whatever we were doing, put on our padded head cover, and run to the shelter, carrying a few hard biscuits in our pockets for emergencies.

The bombing of the city intensified, and I decided if I was going to die, I would rather be with my family when it happened. I moved out of the dormitory and returned to my home. Food shortages and rationing became even more acute as the days progressed. Since my father was spending long hours at work, and I was the only able-bodied youth in my family, I would often go to the country with Kiku to buy some sweet potatoes from farmers. Sweet potatoes were mixed with rice to make gruel to stretch the rationed rice. We even grew pumpkins in our backyard. Sweet potatoes and pumpkins are my favorite vegetables today, although they bring back the distant memory of scarcity in my mind. With well-patrolled seas, foods that had been imported or transported by ship had become extremely scarce. What I missed the most were the fresh bananas that had come from Formosa.

To conserve energy, electricity was only available for a few hours a day, usually for the evening meals. We became quite efficient in planning the cooking time of various foods, stacking up one pot on top of another so that we could cook and warm at the same time. All the windows were covered with dark cloths at night to avoid being spotted from the sky, but I was never afraid. I remember being in a continued state of crisis with adrenalin surging through my body.

I'm a samurai's daughter. I am not afraid. This thought was imprinted in my mind. My family usually gathered in one room; my sister and I did our homework by candlelight, and we went to bed early. I discovered a way to iron handkerchiefs "au naturel" by pasting the wet handkerchief on a window and peeling it off when dry—the most efficient and perfect method. The war years were truly a learning time for us privileged city children. We learned to make use of every scrap of food and other materials, or to go without many, many things that we had thought were so essential to our lives until then.

Luckily, we had a well with a hand pump just outside of our kitchen, so we always had plenty of water for bath and laundry if the tap water were stopped temporarily. Little did we realize that, many months later, that well would save our home from destruction by fire.

Tokyo in Charred Rubble

In the spring of 1945, the intensity and frequency of the firebombing of Tokyo increased. On March 9, one day after my eighteenth birthday, 334 B-29s made a major attack on the city, and eighty-four thousand lives were lost. Thousands of homes were reduced to ashes. As before, we in the suburbs watched from a safe distance. Searchlights frantically crisscrossed the sky, and the moment an aircraft was caught in them, the antiaircraft guns responded with deafening noise. When there was a hit, the cheers went up from our neighborhood.

The next day on my way to school, I saw skeletons of concrete buildings and scarred, stubby, leafless trees still smoldering. In the American mind, the final chapter of World War II was defined by the bombings of Hiroshima and Nagasaki. But for the Japanese, there was an earlier horrendous chapter—the unceasing firebombing in the spring of 1945 of Tokyo, Osaka, and other major cities. I am forever grateful that the ancient cities of Nara (circa 701) and Kyoto (circa 805) were spared.

One windy night in May, the attack began as it had on so many previous nights with the wailing sound of air-raid sirens ever so urgently warning us, followed by the low rumbling sound of the B-29 bombers then the shrill whistling cries of the falling firebombs, the earth shaking, the blinding light of fireballs at impact.

But this night was different. The action was closer than usual. This was not the night to be watching the bombing from our second-floor bedroom windows. We got dressed more carefully, putting on layers of clothes and wearing gloves and sturdy shoes. At our gate, we watched the voracious fire advancing toward us.

Just ahead of the fire, we saw a sea of people running up the road that ran in front of our house on the way to the field at the Tai-iku Gakko (the physical education college). Women, children, and elderly people who had been burned out of their homes were running away from the fire. Pandemonium ensued, everyone pushing and shouting, "Go to the field before the fire overtakes us!" Lost children cried for their mothers, and frantic mothers searched for their children, calling out their names as the hissing sound of the firebombs and the crackling sound of houses burning came closer and closer. Lights had gone out long ago, and the sky was pitch dark, except for the place where the red sky reflected the inferno below.

My father gathered all the able-bodied neighbors and formed a bucket brigade from our well to the road. We took turns pumping the well and splashed water on the houses that faced the path of the advancing fire. The sparks flew as the wind whipped around and the crackling sound of the burning wood came nearer. We pumped and pumped until we felt as if our arms were going to drop out of their sockets, yet, we continued. The house across the road began to burn. We braced ourselves for the worst.

Suddenly the wind shifted. The fire that had been advancing toward us began to move sideways. The hordes of shouting and pushing people had gone to the Taiiku Gakko field, and there remained only those of us in the neighborhood who had valiantly fought to protect our homes. We sat by the road bedraggled and exhausted as the fire receded from us and helplessly watched the fire move away from us, devouring houses one after another in its path. Disheveled, with smudged faces, some of us cried in each other's arms, and others just sat there numb, as if shell-shocked. My father gathered the family, and we gave thanks that we had been spared and mourned others' losses.

As the dawn neared, the bombers retreated. The lifting of the air-raid alert hollowly rang out over the smoldering city. When the first ray of the sun appeared over the horizon, I felt a strong appreciation for life. However hopeless life may seem, there was a magical power in the dawn's early light. That night, our heroic efforts to save our homes from the fire showed me the near-inexhaustible capacity of humans in times of crisis; when the body gives up, the mind takes over.

With the immediate danger past, my father instructed us to cook all the rice we had and make rice balls for the neighbors who'd lost their homes. Then he had us fill the bathtub with water pumped from the well, heat it with firewood, and invited them to take a hot bath. Over forty people came to take the bath at our house that day.[1]

My father instructed me to get on my bicycle and check our grandparents' house a few miles away. There were no trains, no buses, no electricity, no gas, no phone, and no water. The city had stopped. I pedaled through streets with charred remains of houses on either side still smoldering. A few people were poking around with sticks to see what they could salvage. To my relief, I found my grandparents and their home unharmed, but most of the neighborhood was in pain. I pedaled through Koshukaido, a major highway where I used to take the trolley to go to my school. The main thoroughfare, normally busy with trolleys and buses, was now deserted. I was shocked to see the devastation that razed our city for miles. If some buildings were standing, they were half crumbled. The leafless trees were scorched painfully. I went to see Yoshiko, my best friend, a tall slender girl with beautiful, large, dewy eyes. I found her standing forlornly on the site where her magnificent home had once stood. Sometimes we had played duets on her grand piano. But now the piano was no more. We hugged without a word and cried in each other's arms. Her family had escaped with literally only their clothes on their backs.

On the way home, I happened to spot Masako, another classmate, trying to build a fire to cook some rice gruel beside a makeshift lean-to of some scrap tinplates. She and her family, too, were lucky to be alive. Under the viaduct, I saw motionless bodies, perhaps seeking refuge from the fire last night. Suddenly I was overcome with the emotions that had been swirling around inside of me: anger, despair, and sadness. I felt so very tired that I just wanted to drop to the ground and sleep and not ever wake up.

---

[1]   A Japanese bath is very hot, and we wash and rinse outside of the tub; the tub is used only for soaking.

11

PICTORIAL

1ST PRIZE: Richard S. Ikei, Tokyo Area Engr, Teikoku Seimei Bldg., APO 181.

2ND PRIZE: T/4 Charles B. Renaud, Office of the Chief Surgeon GHQ AFAC, APO 500.
Sgt. R. L. Steven.

3RD PRIZE: Lt. P. S. Jackson, Legal Section GHQ, SCAP.
Pfc. Joe Yamada, APO 502, ATIS GHQ.
Jaya Murti.

HUMAN INTEREST

1ST PRIZE: T/5 Bracey Holt Jr., AG Records GHQ, AFPAC, APO 500.

2ND PRIZE: Lt. Harold Cosel, Hqs. 139 ACS Sq. APO 181.
Pfc. Yamada, APO 500, ATIS, GHQ.

3RD PRIZE: T/5 Richard Witenburg, SAD AFPAC APO 500.
Alvin Melnick, APO 500 GHQ SCAP ESS/IE.
T/4 Chet Defty, APO 181 584 Engr Const Gp.

HONORABLE MENTION

T/4 Charles B. Renaud, Office of the Chief Surgeon GHQ AFPAC APO 500.
Allen Minick, APO 500 GHQ SCAP ESS/IE No. 75 Yuraku Hotel.
Lt. P. S. Jackson, Legal Section GHQ.
Lt. Harold Cosel, HQS 39 ACS Sq APO 181.
Apl, Alfred John Corentevi, RA 39423792 Hq. Co. 54 ECOGF APO 181 C/o P.M S.F. Calf.
T/5 Charles Nantais 584 ENGR Const Gp APO 181.
Alvin Minick, 715 Yuraku Bldg.
Madelene W. Dewey, Room No. 810 Meiji Bldg.

Our friend Bracey won the first place in Human Interest photo.

13

I pulled myself together and began pedaling home. On the way, I saw a young woman with vacant eyes, her hair in complete disarray, mumbling to herself, wandering in the street dressed in tattered clothes, holding a silent baby in her arms. Maybe her house had burnt down. Maybe her baby was dead. I didn't stop to ask or help her. Overwhelmed by so much death and destruction, I longed for my family and hurried home.

My Father in Jail

A few days later, about a dozen military police appeared at our house as if they were on a major manhunt. A couple of somber-looking men guarded our gate, fearing my father might escape! Several men with tightly pursed lips, perhaps to convey the seriousness of the matter, stationed themselves around the yard and by the back gate. We were completely unprepared for this but not surprised. My father had been speaking against the war and the government ever since the war had started. The most important-looking man, who was barking orders to the others, approached my father and told him in an officious voice that he was under suspicion of being a spy.

My father was a man who seldom lost his cool in an adversarial situation. After listening quietly, he told the officer, "I have done nothing to betray my country. I'll be happy to go to the headquarters with you men, as I know I'll be released immediately. You either have the wrong man, or there was some misunderstanding." He instructed my mother to pack a few personal belongings, and with a smile, said, "I shall return in no time. Do not worry." Then he was driven in the police car to Sugamo Prison, where political prisoners were being kept.

We three girls gathered around our mother looking for an answer. Like my father, my mother had come from a long line of samurai, and in a samurai family, even women learned to control their emotions and not lose their composure in times of crisis. "He'll be back soon," she said comfortingly, half trying to convince herself, and instructed us to go to our rooms and do our homework, telling Kiku to begin dinner preparation.

It was weeks before we heard news about our father. We were notified that he had been transferred to the local jail like a common criminal and was to stay there for an indefinite period of time. When my mother went to see him, she found him in a small, solitary cell about six by six feet.

Many of his friends and colleagues attempted to obtain his release, to no avail. He wrote later in his memoir that he had a revelation in jail: "If you are anxious to leave the prison, you'll be unhappy. But if you stop being anxious to leave, and if you tell yourself that two tatami mats are plenty big enough for one human being, you will not be anxious." (Noritsu-Ichidaiki [History of Efficiency Management], published 1971, Tokyo, Japan)

In such a small place, my father was not getting enough exercise, so he volunteered to clean the prison toilets. He would strip to his waist and kill maggots and scrub the toilets from top to bottom. The warden was dumbfounded to see this distinguished political prisoner lower himself to being a toilet cleaner.

My father answered, "Oh, this is just my exercise. It's nothing."

In his memoir, my father says of his jail stay that even being as tough and resourceful as he was, the army of ticks, lice, and other bedbugs often got the upper hand, robbing him of precious sleep. Every night, he battled the bedbugs, and he became thinner and thinner as the days progressed. The meals were usually brown rice gruel, pickled plums, and radishes, so he sometimes had some food brought in from home. When he was exceptionally tired, he would have the tea ceremony utensils and tea brought from home, and he'd go to the visitor's room and make ceremonial tea to lift his spirits. When the war ended and he was finally released, he had sunken eyes and spindly legs and weighed only ninety-four pounds.

In early August 1945, the enemy planes scattered leaflets from the sky on the crumbling city. One of the guards brought the leaflet and showed it to my father and asked what he thought of it. The leaflet said in Japanese, "The Japanese government is beginning the peace talks. Why do you Japanese citizens want to continue to fight? Surrender!"

My father told the guard, "If, on the radio, the Japanese government does not deny this statement within the next twenty-four hours, I think it is true."

There was no word of denial. My father told the warden and the guards that the war would be over within a week. On August 7, the

United States dropped the atom bomb on Hiroshima, followed by another on Nagasaki.

Surrender

Twelve noon, August 15, 1945 is a time that is etched in the psyche of those Japanese who lived through it. The oppressive, white summer heat seemed to envelop the ravaged capital of Japan and keep the city in silent suspension. We were notified that the emperor was going to speak to the nation at noon. Even the noisy cicadas seemed to have sensed the gravity of the moment and stopped their singing. My family, with my father still in jail, gathered around the radio listening intently.

This was the first time in history that ordinary Japanese citizens would hear the emperor's voice. We had been told that he was divine. In my family, no one held such a belief, but we were filled with awe and apprehension. The high-pitched, tinny voice of the emperor, which sounded like a woman's, came over the radio telling his subjects that Japan had lost a war to a foreign power for the first time in its two thousand six hundred-year history. I heard someone cry out in the neighborhood. The Emperor continued to beseech us to "endure the unbearable" and not to revolt or cause trouble during the American occupation of Japan.

We sat speechless and limp, as if every muscle in our bodies had gone slack.

Tears rolled down everyone's cheeks, and we cried silently. Cicadas resumed their noisy chatter, and the sound of noontime meal preparation in the neighborhood brought us back to reality.

CHAPTER II: THE *MESSIAH* CHORUS

Rising from the Ashes

The summer of 1945 was a confusing and chaotic time for us ordinary Japanese citizens. We knew we had lost the war, but we really didn't know what was to come. There was a rumor that American soldiers were going to rape all the women and kill or maim the men. In fact, many families sent their daughters to country cousins or to other places far away from the city. My father, who was still in jail, told us through mother, who visited him, that from his experience in the United States, American men were gentlemen and we needed not fear.

It was rumored that, Japanese on the coast of Kyushu, the southernmost island of Japan where the American occupation forces were expected to land, were arming themselves with bamboo spears to fight Americans to the death. My family, including my sister Aiko, who was home from the country, spent each day filled with apprehension in the hot and humid city.

Those were the darkest hours in Japanese history. After the emperor had addressed the nation, the docile Japanese took his words to heart and obeyed all the rules and restrictions handed down by General MacArthur with nary a whimper. Being accustomed for thousands of years to a life of scarcity in a nation of few natural resources, *gaman* (endure) and *gambaru* (persistence) were the two words that were valued and drummed into every Japanese child from birth. Guided by those values and being industrial by nature, the citizens set to work cleaning and rebuilding the ravaged cities.

Amid the rubble of bombed-out buildings and blackened, leafless trees that stretched throughout Tokyo as far as the eye could see, hastily assembled shanties, made of tinplates and salvaged boards, dotted the cityscape of Tokyo, once the thriving capital of Japan. Here and there, white porcelain toilets shone eerily. (Japanese houses are built of wood and burn easily. After the houses were burnt down, porcelain, which does not burn, was left.) In the evening, narrow ribbons of white smoke from cooking fires would softly rise into the sky.

Little by little, the rubble disappeared, and the trees began to sprout leaves. The sunken cheeks of the survivors began to have more human color, and the women, still in their drab dark slacks and blouses, began to fuss with their hair and wear lipstick again. I was back in school. This time, I was not ashamed to open English books on the train, and I did not have to work in the munitions factory after class. These were both scary and exhilarating days for those of us who studied English, because, hey, we knew the enemy language.

Tsudajuku Univ., Circa 1944. Faith in rear.

Tsud Juku Univ.

Wood-burning taxis. Bracey and me.

General MacArthur coming out of GHQ in Tokyo, circa 1945.

With the American occupation, our food supplies seemed to improve somewhat. From the military we got such rare commodities as flour, sugar, margarine—we'd never seen this butter substitute before—and split peas to make soup.

The well-fed and smartly dressed GIs in uniform, zipping along the burned out streets of Tokyo in their jeeps, became a common sight. To the dismay of thoughtful Japanese adults, throngs of innocent children ran after these big, smiling soldiers, who generously gave out chewing gum and candies that were treated with awe like rare treasures. Even some long-deprived adults would follow the GIs for cigarettes and other handouts.

At Ginza, Tokyo's major intersection, a throng of wide-eyed and open-mouthed Japanese watched the spit-and-polish MPs on a platform direct traffic with the flourish and drama of ballet dancers. To the Japanese, policemen and soldiers were supposed to be serious and somber.

Making Do with What We Got: Wood-burning Taxis

While the Japanese watched aghast at the American MPs in Ginza, the Americans watched with equal bewilderment a peculiar postwar spectacle: wood-burning taxis! After the war, we didn't even have enough fuel to run automobiles, but the innovative Japanese came up with a wood-burning fuel that could move taxis. I don't know the mechanics of it, but the taxis had a contraption on the back of the car that burned wood chips spewing smoke as they sped through the city. We didn't care whether the fuel was gasoline or wood, so long as the taxis got us where we wanted to go.

Save Yamashita!

Around December 1945, my father, who had been released from jail, read in the paper about the trial by the Allied Forces of General Yamashita. Yamashita was to be tried as a war criminal, and a death sentence was impending. My father was shocked that no Japanese had protested against the general's death sentence, when only a short time before he had been worshipped as the country's greatest patriot and hero.

My father was outraged at the spineless apathy of his countrymen. He gathered his office staff and told them that he was going to protest.

Everyone advised him against such a reckless act. "Please don't do anything foolish; you'll be seen as a military sympathizer and end up in jail again. The future of our institute will be endangered," his colleagues and friends pleaded.

"The fact that I was put in jail by the Japanese military government proves I'm not a military sympathizer. I need to talk to General MacArthur and tell him he is making a mistake," he insisted.

My father was a true patriot in the sense that he did not blindly support his country but saw things objectively and criticized the government when he felt it had failed the people's trust. He did not want anyone to think that the Japanese were a spineless people. Against everyone's objection, he ripped off the curtains in our drawing room and made a huge banner and wrote in bold letters with a Japanese writing brush:

> *I am not trying to save our military. I am not a relative or friend of General Yamashita. I am just an ordinary citizen of Japan. General Yamashita fought the war as a patriot and soldier to do his job. Do you remember how we applauded his victories in the news? He now faces death at the hands of the occupied forces. Are we to stand by silently and allow this great human being to be put to death? I'm going to General MacArthur with 10,000 signatures to petition for the release of General Yamashita. Let the United States hear the righteous voice of our nation! I'll take full responsibility. Please sign!*[2]

He put the banner up in the middle of burned-out Ginza, the Fifth Avenue of Tokyo, where he stood on an orange crate and called out to the passersby. A crowd formed, and many, touched by his sincerity, signed. An old woman left some money and bowed in Buddhist prayers. Three men signed with their blood. Another knocked the table over cursing my father as a "military sympathizer!"

Middle-aged men and young women were in favor of the release, and young men were against it. The *United Press* photographer and other

---

[2]   *History of Efficiency Management*, 1955.

news media people began to gather. An American GI stopped to ask what it was all about, and after listening to my father's explanation in English, he said, "That's good," and signed his name.[3]

A *UP* correspondent offered to be an intermediary for my father with General MacArthur. My father took seven thousand eight hundred signatures on the petition typed in English to General MacArthur's headquarters, where he was met by Chief of Staff General Sutherland. My father told him:

"General Yamashita only did the job expected of a soldier. If he is sentenced to death simply because he helped in the war effort, I should be sentenced too as I helped to design a warplane to help win the war. In fact most of the Japanese should be sentenced to death as we all helped in the war effort."

"That is not the reason for his death sentence," General Sutherland replied. "It is because he was responsible for the deaths of 50,000 civilians in the Philippines."

After a brief meeting, my father was invited to have some tea with the staff. This was a golden opportunity for him, having been a soapbox orator since his youth.

"It was a great mistake for Japan to enter into this war," my father began. "Japan had never prepared herself for a war with the United States. All of our war preparation was aimed at Russia. We have never practiced battle against America. Our military men are studying about Russia. General Yamashita had wanted to advise the Emperor to stop the war, but he was obstructed by General Tojo. So General Yamashita is not a warmonger, but since he is a soldier, he simple did his job well. Besides, there are few authorities on Russia as good as General Yamashita today. The United States is a rich country and can make any kind of weapons you want to, but human knowledge and experience built over many years could not be bought with any amount of money. It would be a great loss to lose a man of Yamashita's caliber."

---

[3]   Ibid, 129.

Some of the American staff said, "That's true. Yamashita is a great authority on Russia." Not missing this opportunity, my father eloquently added,

"That's right. That is why you shouldn't kill Yamashita. I'm sure there will come a time when the United States will face off with Russia. To have someone like Yamashita with such extraordinary knowledge and experience with Russia would be a great benefit to you!"[4]

After this meeting, my father was called in for questioning by the Counter Intelligence Department several times, his friends and business associates were checked, his bank accounts were investigated to make sure he was not a right-wing agitator.

In spite of his effort, however, General Yamashita was sentenced to death by hanging.

Destiny

AMERICAN-JAPANESE CHORUS. A chorus of 250 Americans and Japanese, accompanied by the 75-piece Tokyo Philharmonic orchestra, is pictured here broadcasting Handel's Messiah Sunday night over station WVTR, Tokyo. The same group will present the Messiah at 7 p.m. Christmas night at Hibiya Park auditorium. (Signal Corps Photo by Sgt. Edward J. Pitra)

---

4   Ibid, 129–130.

December 22nd & 23rd

at

Tokyo Imperial University Auditorium

and

December 25th

Tokyo Hibiya-Park Public Hall

*　*　*　*　*

Handel's

MESSIAH

American & Japanese Christian Chorus

accompanied by

The Nippon Philharmonic Orchestra

*　*　*　*　*

Rev. Ugo Nakada ··· ··· ··· ··· ··· ··· ··· ··· ···Director

Mrs. Minako Hirai ··· ··· ··· ··· ··· ··· ··· ··· ···Soprano

Miss Kiyo Kono··· ··· ··· ··· ··· ··· ··· ··· ··· ···Alto

T/4 Dallas Taggert ··· ··· ··· ··· ··· ··· ··· ··· ···Bass

Mr. Seiichi Sonoda ··· ··· ··· ··· ··· ··· ··· ··· ···Tenor

Pvt. Howard B. Phillipy ··· ··· ··· ··· ··· ··· ··· ···Bass

Mr. Keikichi Sonoda ··· ··· ··· ··· ··· ··· ··· ··· ···Bass

Miss June Nakada ··· ··· ··· ··· ··· ··· ··· ··· ···Pianist

Pvt. David Larson ··· ··· ··· ··· ··· ··· ··· ··· ···Pianist

Mr. Toshiaki Okamoto ··· ··· ··· ··· ··· ··· ··· ···Organist

In the fall of 1945, my friends and I saw a notice on the school bulletin board recruiting female voices for a United States/Japan-combined chorus that would sing the *Messiah* at Christmas. This idea, we were told, was General MacArthur's. His goal was to build goodwill between the victor and the vanquished, but they lacked female voices and tapped women's universities in Tokyo. A few of my classmates and I decided that this was a golden opportunity to practice English with native speakers, and we signed up. Under the baton of Reverend Nakada, we met at Tokyo University every week for practice. It was a large chorus of two hundred fifty American GIs and Japanese college students.

My friends and I began to pay more attention to our looks. In the burned-out city, scarcity of clothing stores was a chronic problem. My mother, with two teenage daughters at home, did many ingenious things to keep us decently dressed. She procured white silk fabric from the military that was used for army parachutes and made us pretty blouses. She got hold of wool fabric that was used for navy signal flags—bright yellow, green, and red—and made us smart-looking coats and suits. We got shoes on the black market. To an optimistic eighteen-year-old, our defeat in the war did not seem that bad, and times were certainly better than they'd been during the war. Possibilities seemed to lurk just around the corner.

On December 25, 1945, the day of the concert finally arrived. We gathered at Hibiya Public Hall, one of the few performance buildings still standing in the city. A few days earlier, we had broadcast throughout Japan over WVTR from the Tokyo University's auditorium, accompanied by the Japan Philharmonic Orchestra.

Once the GIs discovered that they could communicate with us in English, they would spontaneously strike up a conversation, something Japanese men did not do.

"So, what university do you go to?

"How do you know English?"

"Where do you live?"

They were very friendly and curious, and they smiled a lot. It was a different custom from ours, in which strangers didn't smile or talk to each other. The photos of smiling Americans and my father during his student days in Ohio kept flashing through my mind. Here they were, the genuine things, and they didn't disappoint me.

The concert was a great success. Our cheeks flushed from the excitement and happiness of having performed well, everyone gathered in small clusters to say good-bye. I had told my father that I had joined a United States/Japan-combined chorus, and he had given me his full support and encouragement, adding, "Those soldiers must be very homesick thousands of miles away from home, just as I was when I was a student in Ohio, and the people there were so kind to me. I want to repay their hospitality. Why don't you invite them to our home for a Christmas party?"

For as long as I can remember, we had always decorated a Christmas tree, probably a custom my father brought back from America, and my parents would give us books as presents. I think this was fairly uncommon in Japanese homes then. Today, some Japanese families decorate small Christmas trees for their festiveness.

After the concert, I asked my classmates and several GIs who were gathered around me, "Who would like to come to a Christmas party at my home?"

Everyone said, "Me!"

We piled on to a weapons carrier and sped through the dark streets to my home in a suburb of Tokyo. My parents gave the visitors a most warm, cordial welcome. The GIs had to remove their shoes at the entrance, their first Japanese culture experience. They walked gingerly in their stocking feet, taking care not to bump their heads on the low threshold, probably feeling like Gulliver on the island of Lilliput. They were surprised and pleased to see a Christmas tree. My mother had prepared a light supper for us, and afterward, we played the piano, sang, talked, and had a grand time.

Meeting My Future Husband

A week went by, and I thought no more about the Christmas party. One day, two handsome young GIs came knocking at our door. Earle and Bracey were among the group of soldiers who had come to our Christmas party. We marveled at their "homing instinct" in finding our house through bombed-out streets without names. They both had the well-scrubbed look of an "all-American Christian boy": handsome and courteous, yet ready for a good time. Earle was an eighteen-year-old college student from Illinois, with blue gray twinkling eyes, medium build, and a head full of soft, wavy, light brown hair piled high in the pompadour style of the time.

With an *r* and an *l* in Earl's name, my family could not pronounce it, and since, to our amazement, he ate raw carrots like a rabbit, which was never done in Japan, we renamed him "Bunny-san" (Mr. Bunny Rabbit).

His buddy, Bracey, from Tennessee, another eighteen-year-old college freshman from Tennessee, had light brown hair and large, hazel eyes and had a habit of gesturing with his hand a lot. "Bracey" was more manageable than "Earle," but came out somewhat Japanized to "Bu-leh-shii-san." Both were music majors in college and had been drafted just as the war was winding down and sent to Japan after a few months of training camp. Bracey aspired to become a concert pianist. The love of music helped to forge a close bond among us. The two became frequent visitors to our home. Sometimes they brought their friends and some records, and we would have a dance party!

Changing Japan

The defeat of Japan shook the Japanese psyche to its foundation. It seemed that everything we believed in until that time had been a lie. There was an old Japanese saying, *Ka-te-ba Kangun, Ma-ke-re-ba Zoku-gun* (The victor is righteous and the vanquished, evil).

We wanted to rid ourselves of the old militarism that had led the nation to an unprecedented disaster and tragedy. American democracy seemed to us like a shining beacon. Even our great cultural heritage of which we were so proud seemed tarnished. Just as Japan had changed in 1867 from the feudal shogun regime to a monarchy fashioned after Great Britain, in 1946 Japan embraced *De-mo-ku-ra-shii*, fashioned after the American style of government. The Japanese had always been an adaptable people. Over many centuries, the Japanese had taken from foreign cultures what worked for them and merged it into their own culture. From the turn of the century, men started to wear business suits and shoes to work, but once at home changed into kimono to relax. We borrowed the British educational system. Since the Japanese are pantheistic and polytheistic and do not have the kind of restrictive religious beliefs as Muslims and Christians and other faiths do, such adaptations took place without much ado.

Can Blue Eyes See the Same?

Until the end of the Pacific War in 1945, Caucasians in the city of Tokyo were rare, and to most Japanese, the tall, white, hairy Americans with different colors of eyes and hair were an amazing sight. The Japanese are like native Americans and do not grow much body hair, and all Japanese have the same color of hair and eyes—black or close to it.

One day, Earle happened to be visiting us while our gardener was tending the garden. Watching Earle intently, the gardener whispered to my father, "These American don't have any color in their eyes. Do you suppose they can see as well as we can?" He couldn't imagine how blue, gray, or green eyes could possible see the world in the same way the Japanese eyes could.

CHAPTER III: "Who Won the War?"

"Faith," a new name

In the old Japan, people were more polite and formal than they are today. Even among family members, we addressed one another with terms of respect such as *san* just as they did in the American south long ago, such as "Miss Mary," or "Master John." The only person in my family who would call me "Nobuko" without any honorifics was my father. So when GIs addressed me as "Nobuko," it offended me.

One day Earle asked me, "Is there a meaning in your name?"

I told him, "the Child of Faith. When my parents married, they vowed to love, honor, and have faith in each other and they named their three daughters, Keiko (child of honor), Nobuko (child of faith) and Aiko (child of love)."

"What a beautiful story," Earle proclaimed. "May I call you 'Faith' from now on?"

The name stuck. When I became a U.S. citizen, I made it my official name.

Learning Each Other's Cultures

My family loved the easy way Earle interacted with every member of our family, totally unafraid of my father, but still respectful. I liked his winking—a nonexistent custom in Japan. His every demeanor captured my heart. He was never afraid to try new food and experiences. He became an instant aficionado of sushi. As Tokyo slowly rose from the ashes, some of the entertainment that flourished before the war began to return. We introduced him to his first ballet and opera performances.

One day, Earle brought a game called *Monopoly*. We would spend hours learning and playing this most typically American game. Especially in the winter, we would all sit around the *kotatsu*, a charcoal hearth dug into the floor with a wooden table over it, and buy and sell Boardwalk and Pennsylvania Avenues, Earle winning and mother losing every time.

Poison Fish Test

Father sampled Fugu first.

One day, my father decided Earle should have the ultimate test of Japanese gastronomic bravery, and he took the whole family to a fugu (blowfish) restaurant. In Japan, a chef must be trained and licensed by the government to prepare fugu, as it is one of the deadliest fish in the ocean. A certain part the fish is poisonous, and even the tiniest mistake in cutting the fish could result in the instant death of the eater. Even though a handful of people in Japan still die every year from eating fugu prepared by unlicensed chefs, Japanese men are drawn to fugu for its exquisite taste and a sense of danger.

We all sat around the low table in a private Japanese room at the fugu restaurant, and my father explained the history of fugu eating. A large dish with small, thin, transparent pieces of fugu arranged like the petals of a chrysanthemum flower was brought in. My father said in a solemn tone, "Wait, I'll be the taster first."

We all watched solemnly in silence. He didn't die.

We had a great fugu dinner. Earle didn't know what to make of this strange custom—he wasn't sure whether my father was putting on an act, or whether it was truly a Japanese custom for the father to risk his life for his guests!

Japanese Hot Spring Adventure

Earle was a gentle young man and spoke of his mother often. My mother said, "A man who is kind to his mother is a good man."

My father liked him because he was a wide-eyed country boy willing to try exotic customs. He was a nonsmoking, nondrinking, non-swearing boy who was the president of the Baptist Youth Fellowship back in Illinois. We all sort of adopted him and his equally sweet and innocent buddy, Bracey, as members of our family and took them everywhere.

When we took Earle and Bracey to a Japanese *onsen* (hot spring), we forgot to give them "*onsen* orientation," an explanation of hot spring custom. You can imagine their shock as, while they soaked in the huge Roman bath, naked Japanese women walked in without even a glance at them. In the olden days at a hot spring resort, men and women had separate changing areas but shared the large pool-size bath. Even in smaller hot spring baths, it was not unusual for a whole family to take a bath together.

Who Won the War?

By the spring of 1946, Earle and I were sure we were destined to be together. One Sunday, Earle asked to speak to my father alone, and he respectfully popped the question of our marriage. I put my ear to the door and listened to see how this was going to develop. As far as my father was concerned, Earle was a nice boy, but still "wet behind the ears," and a student to boot. How was he going to support his wife in the style she was accustomed to? "Too young," he said. He had no problem with Earle being an American. The talk got heated, but my father would not budge.

The dinner table that night was unusually glum without conversations. The news traveled fast, and my elder sister and her husband came to express their sympathy and console me. My mother, my sisters, and even my brother-in-law all worked on my father for months until he finally relented.

Many years after my father had passed away, I read one of his books written in 1921 in which he predicted the future war between Japan and the United States. He wrote: "In order to avoid such a war, Japanese and Americans should intermarry." Had I known this, I could have presented Earle and my union as the forging of a bond between the two countries he loved.

Letter to My Future Mother-in-law

Other obstacles lay before us. The new president of the United States, Mr. Harry S. Truman, issued an edict that the American servicemen could not marry Japanese women. An old letter I wrote to Earle's mother of our resolve turned up fifty years later:

Dear Mrs. Barcus,

*Thank you very much for your nice and kind letter. I got it a
few days before Earle's birthday. We spent his birthday at the room
of my aunt's house that we had rented to live after the marriage,
and we invited three boys and two girls. It was not a big party,
however, we enjoyed it very much. We had nice Sukiyaki, (this is a
favorite food of Japanese, and most Americans like it too). We made
a circle around the 'hibachi' (Japanese stove that burns smokeless
charcoal), put the pan of Sukiyaki, which contains chopped carrots,
onions, turnips, and the roots of some kind of plant. Oh, I forgot to
tell you that we have to have meat (usually beef), and if we go to
the butcher and say "give me the meat for*

*Dream Journey, 1922, page 80

*Sukiyaki," he will make many slices with fat. At first we put
the fat in the pan, then vegetables and meat, adding the 'Shoyu'
(bean sauce) and sugar. By this time it's ready to eat, I would say,
and everybody took their chopsticks and dove into the pan. You will
imagine the scene that followed after that; there was left an empty
pan, and the girls had to put the mixture again. I don't remember
how many times we emptied the pan that night. We had rice
instead of bread, because it goes very well with sukiyaki. We had
martinis with olives for a toast before the meal. This day was Al's
birthday also, (Earle's friend) and downstairs my aunt's family was
having a party for her daughter's birthday. We had three birthdays
at one time in one house, so we ate and played till 11:00 o'clock.

As we had two rooms upstairs, boys slept in the small Japanese
style-room and the girls occupied the big room in spite of the fact
that the girls were fewer than the boys. I would like to make good
Sukiyaki for you when I come there, and I bet you love it. I suppose
Earle has told you already about the order that was issued at the end
of January so we can not marry for a while, maybe till the end of
this year. However we shall keep our engagement on just like before,
because we know how much we need each other in the future. I
feel that this is our fate which was given from God. You may think
it's a silly idea. I have such an idea which I thought out from my
experiences (although they are a little). It's that, God won't give us
any trial we cannot endure. He only gives us the hard trial to the*

35

people whom He thinks are strong enough to bear. We promised to be together, and he has never broken the promise, and I too. For this, my family and the friends will encourage us. Now I suppose I better close because my hand is as tired as your eyes. Please give my best regards to dear Mr. Barcus and your family.

Sincerely, Faith

I illustrated in pen and ink the scenes of our Sukiyaki party and how we slept on the Tatami floor. The long-forgotten letter turned up while the family was cleaning out my father-in-law's house after he died. I was pleasantly surprised at the level of my English skills then and at how religious I had been. I was also touched by our innocence, unimaginable in today's promiscuous environment.

The Wedding

In 1947, President Truman changed his mind, and we were finally able to get married. By that time, my father had changed his mind also, and he planned for us the finest wedding that was possible at that time of scarcity. As was the case for most Japanese, my family had no affiliations with any particular religions, and we chose a lovely chapel at the Seiroka (St. Luke's) Hospital.

The Japanese are not particularly religious people, at least not in the way other peoples of the world are. Whether Shinto or Buddhist, the practice is loosely organized, without the weekly worship Christians have or the daily bowing to Allah Islamists adhere to. Japanese have no compunction about getting married in a Christian church for effect then blessed by the Shinto priest. But all Japanese are buried in the Buddhist rituals.

My mother designed and made my wedding gown with white silk brocade. It was a modest wedding compared to weddings of today, but it seemed very grand to me. Earle's friend, Woody, was our best man and my younger sister, Aiko, was a bridesmaid. We had an afternoon reception at St. Paul's Club in downtown Tokyo, where my family and friends and Earle's office friends mingled easily.

In the Occupied Japan, Earle and I needed a lot of permissions from his superior officers to do anything together. Also, as we were a few months short of twenty-one, we needed permissions from our parents to marry, even from Earle's superiors who tried their best to dissuade him.

They say love is blind. It blinds a person from making sane judgments. I was so intoxicated by the romantic notion of being a wife of a handsome, young man that I wanted to be a full-time wife and dropped out of the college of my dream.

CHAPTER IV:
THE SEED OF MY AMERICAN JOURNEY: MY FATHER'S AMERICAN EXPERIENCE

The Beginning

Many things shape a person's destiny. Birthplace, parents, schooling, environment, and events, large and small and often beyond one's control, propel us to become who we are. The Pacific War was a major event in my life. For my father, his experience in America in the early twentieth century had a strong impact on his future career success and on his life philosophy, which, in turn, affected us three daughters. Powerful and unexpected events that followed his studies in America helped to germinate the seed of my American journey and helped that seed to grow into a mighty tree, taking me to unimaginable paths along the way.

In 1918, when my father was twenty-three years old and working in a research lab at Fujikura Densen Company, he received a scholarship from the Japanese Ministry of Agriculture and Commerce to study rubber chemistry at Akron University in Ohio. In the early twentieth century, Japan was sending their best and brightest abroad, mostly to the United States and England, to learn the technology that was lacking in Japan.

My father's big black steamer trunk that followed him to America was stored in our attic and filled with memories of his student days in Ohio. When I was a child, I used to explore in the dark, musty attic alone and was drawn to colorful stickers with foreign names I could not read. In the trunk, I found yellowed photographs of my father's student days in Ohio from 1918 to 1921 and books and letters written in a language unfamiliar to me. The photos of the white houses with white picket fences seemed like houses in fairy tales in my child's mind, especially compared to the somber, unpainted houses hidden behind tall fences in my neighborhood.

The tall, hairy, fair-colored people with big noses who mingled with my small father, with his thick, black hair—all smiling happily—fascinated me. In the old Japan, we did not smile when photographed. Showing teeth in public was considered vulgar. To me, these smiling foreigners appeared to be so happy and friendly.

I discovered later that *Dream Journey*, a chronicle of my father's study in America published in Japan in 1922, is filled with humorous anecdotes. For example, the custom of tipping, the ladies-first culture (especially interesting coming from the perspective of the men-first culture of Japan at that time), and the serving of a glass of ice water at a restaurant in the dead of winter all seemed quite peculiar to my father. He loved the way Americans didn't stand on ceremony. He admired their independent spirit, boldness, and keen sense of humor—the very essence of my father. In Americans he found a kindred spirit, and his experience in the United States became a turning point in his life. Half a century later, it led to my American journey.

He wrote in his memoir:

As soon as a woman stepped into the elevator, the Caucasian man next to me took off his hat, and three other men followed suit. Ahhh, this is what I read about in the guidebook that, in America, when you address a woman or just to greet her, men must take their hats off. It also said men may not smoke without the woman's permission! * (*Dream Journey*)

He had read and heard about Americans' efficient way of doing things and about their open-mindedness to change and to embracing new technology. At every turn, he was impressed with this American "nothing ventured, nothing gained" philosophy, the philosophy he instilled in us girls as we were growing up.

*Dream Journey, published 1922, page 8

Crossing the continent by train from California to Ohio simply blew my father's mind away. He had never seen anything so gigantic. The mountains, plains, deserts, pastures, wheat fields, rivers, forests, and trees were all beyond any human scale he had known back in Japan. I would have the same reaction forty years later when I arrived in 1948 and crossed the United States by train from Seattle to Chicago.

At the university, my father discovered a new field called industrial engineering that was nonexistent in Japan then. He decided that this particular field was the difference between America and Japan in their levels of industrial development. Japan had no overall national plan; nor did the country have the tools to create such a plan.

My father also learned about a new field of efficiency; time and motion study was a scientific management technique spearheaded by a man named Frank Gilbreth. He thought these two fields, industrial engineering and efficiency, were the keys to the great industrial growth in the United States and wanted to introduce them to Japan to help her grow. After finishing his program at Akron University, he went to Boston to study at Mr. Gilbreth's Time and Motion laboratory at the Massachusetts Institute of Technology. Mr. Gilbreth had died, and his wife, Lillian, was continuing her husband's pioneering work while raising twelve children. (Later a story about raising their family using the efficiency method would be made into a movie titled *Cheaper by the Dozen*.).

While at the laboratory, my father stayed with a family named Wheeler in Brookline, the suburb of Boston where I would settle with my family thirty-eight years later.

In 1922, armed with his graduate degree from the Akron University, full of new ideas, hopes, and dreams, he set up an office in Tokyo and called it Araki Efficiency Management Institute. But Japan in the 1920s was not quite ready to open up to his "radical" innovation. It had only been fifty years since Japan had emerged from a feudal era and the men had stopped wearing topknots and carrying swords. The people were still deeply steeped in the old ways. Words such as "efficiency" and "industrial management" were alien concepts to an ancient tradition where "function followed form," just the opposite of the American way.

41

The Great Kanto Earthquake as a Matchmaker

While he was struggling to establish his new business, my father's old high school buddy introduced him to my mother, a shy, beautiful young woman with dreamy eyes. My father, a handsome and debonair young man just back from America who would open doors for the ladies, was the talk of the neighborhood. It didn't take long for these two young people to fall in love.

As a prospective husband for women from good homes, my father had a few strikes against him. First, he had no parents, a serious handicap in the Japanese society of old. In addition, his two older sisters were unmarried; belonged to SEITO, a new feminist organization whose members were known to imbibe; and one had a child out of wedlock. My maternal grandfather, a naval officer, was dead set against my mother marrying this brash, Americanized young man with equally unconventional sisters. But my father was confident that there would be an opportunity to prove his worth as a suitor to my mother. He was a man who never gave up once he made up his mind.

My parents did not have to wait long. On September 1, 1923, the Great Kanto Earthquake struck Tokyo. My father rushed to my mother's home to see if their house was unharmed and set to work cleaning out the debris. My grandfather was duly impressed by his devotion. Six months later, they were married in earthquake-shattered Tokyo in a simple ceremony. In an old photo of their ceremony, my mother in traditional Japanese bridal hairstyle and kimono, my father in a tuxedo, and my grandparents and relatives looked quite somber, as if they were attending a funeral. But in the olden days in Japan, nobody ever smiled in the photos.

Around the World in 33 Days!

My parents struggled to keep my father's new business afloat. The financial responsibility grew exponentially with the arrival of their first child, my sister, in 1925, followed two years later by me. At one point, they could not meet the payroll of the office staff, and my mother's Singer sewing machine from America came to the rescue—she sewed the men's shirts as part of their pay.

In 1928, when I was one year old, a remarkable and unexpected event changed my parents' lives. A major newspaper of that time, *Jiji Shimpo*, sponsored a race around the world, like the one taken by Nellie Bly in 1889 in seventy-two days, six hours, eleven minutes, and fourteen seconds. The purpose was to promote goodwill and to awaken the citizens of Japan from feudalistic and provincial thinking to more international awareness.

When my mother saw the notice in the paper, she believed that my father was the one to win this race and encouraged him to apply, but he felt he had no time for such adventure. She secretly sent in the application, thinking that winning such a race by using his efficiency method would help earn recognition for his new business. When the newspaper contacted him, my father was finally convinced of the merits of this race, both as a goodwill ambassador, a concept very dear to his heart, and as a booster for his new business. He took the test with several hundred other applicants and was chosen as one of the two final contestants, one to go eastbound and the other to go westbound. Each contestant was to get the signatures of the mayors of the major cities such as New York, London, Paris, and Rome.

Shake hands with Seattle Mayor, Mrs. Landis

像神女の由自及名署其と氏アカーナウ、スムーヱジ長市育紐

— 111 —

Greetings from James Walker, New York Mayor.

紐　育

紐育アスホーダルテホ歓迎會前列右より三人目紐育市代理市長マンド氏

話は此の競爭のこと、日本のことの上に賬や
かに花を咲かし、分秒を爭ふコースの途上と
いふ觀念も、いつか湧へかちになる。

◇

市長代理のマンド氏は
「市長は今日は先約の委員會があるのだつ
たが、貴方にお目にかかる手筈にして、一時
間も會の出席をのばしたのです「決して人を
待つた事のない市長」を待たした貴方の腕前
は素晴らしいものですよ」
ヒューモーアの言葉に、私も面會の機を得た
いと思ひたつたが、出帆の時刻が迫つて逢ふ
時間もない。
然しそれ程の好意が、私の競爭のコンデイ

— 116 —

Luncheon at Hotel Astor.　Father 2nd from right

46

THE NEW YORK TIMES, THURSDAY, APRIL 19, 1928.

JAPANESE ARRIVES ON WORLD RACE EAST

After Brief Stay He Sails on Aquitania, Expecting to Cross Rival Near London.

LEFT TOKIO 12 DAYS AGO

He Shows Efficiency in Shaving, Greeting Compatriots and Being Interviewed.

ASKS PUBLIC TO WRITE HIM

And Tell the Difference Between Buddhism and Christianity and How Dry We Are.

Toichiro Araki, 34-year-old Japanese business man, who is the eastbound contestant in a two-man race in opposite directions around the world from Tokio, dropped into New York in a mail plane from San Francisco, via Cleveland, yesterday afternoon half an hour ahead of his schedule, shaved himself in three minutes in the corner of a hangar, dashed by automobile to the Hotel Astor, methodically posed for pictures, answered newspaper men's questions with a patient smile, ate a dinner, met Mayor Walker's representative and climbed aboard the Aquitania, bound for Cherbourg, a few minutes before it sailed.

He left Tokio on April 6, just twelve days ago, a few hours ahead of his competitor, Ryukichi Matsui, another Tokio business man, whose task it was to try to beat Araki's time by girdling the globe in a westerly direction. Matsui was reported completing his journey across Siberia by the Transsiberian Railway yesterday and should pass Araki as he leaves London next week on his way to take the same long railway journey in the reverse direction.

The race is sponsored by the Jiji Shimpo, a Tokio newspaper, and its conditions as set forth in a printed "conspectus" are that the contestants shall use no transportation other than existing rail, steamship, motor or air lines and shall not be allowed to make any special arrangements; they must visit a press association office or a Japanese consulate in the principal cities on the route and they "must," it is specifically asserted, "wear suits of blue serge color and it hats." Each man got $2,000 for is expenses and the first man back to Tokio will win a prize of $1,500 posted by the newspaper. The loser gets $500. No attempt is being made to break the record set by Edward S. Evans and Linton Wells in 1926 when they circled the globe in twenty-eight days and fourteen hours. The purpose of the Japanese race, it is declared, is merely to show how quickly and cheaply one may travel around the world using only established means of travel.

Typical of Japanese interest in foreign customs was a list of questions which Araki handed to newspaper men with a request that they be transmitted to the American public and that answers be sent him in care of the Jiji Shimpo at Tokio.

"Please don't take these too seriously," he said, "and if some are found unsuitable, do not mind that."

The questions follow:

To whomsoever this may come: Please be kind enough to help me to understand certain conditions and problems in the United States, in my hurried trip across the country, by answering any or all of the following questions:

Religion.

1. Why does Christian Science prevail to such an extent in the United States?
2. What differences are there between Buddhism and Christianity?

Politics.

3. Why the program of navy extension in the United States?
4. Why do the political parties control the newspapers to such an extent?
5. What are the main issues in the coming Presidential election?

Industry.

6. What is the situation with regard to unemployment in the country?
7. What are the present wages of workingmen, what are the prices of goods?

Sociology.

8. To what extent is the dry law observed?
9. Is it the fashion for ladies to smoke?

Sociology.

8. To what extent is the dry law observed?
9. Is it the fashion for ladies to smoke?

Education.

10. Is there any desire for an international language?
11. Why is the Darwinian theory not taught in the schools?

Oriental Questions.

12. Does the United States want peace in China?
13. Has Japan the right to keep the power in Southern Manchuria?
14. Does this race interest you, in its purpose and its methods?

Thanking you for any answers you may give to these questions, I am, Very respectfully yours,
TOICHIRO ARAKI,
Eastbound contestant, Jiji Shimpo Race,
Tokio, Japan.

Specialized in Industrial Chemistry.

Before he went to the pier to board the Aquitania, Araki came to THE TIMES Annex to pay his respects to the American press and to bring the greetings of the Jiji Shimpo to the staff of THE TIMES. He regretted that he would not have time to go to the movies before leaving

In his education in Japan and here, Araki specialized in industrial chemistry. Returning to Japan in 1922 from his stay in America, he was commissioned by the Government to study industrial efficiency and a year later opened his own office as a consulting engineer for industries following the modern Japanese trend toward "Fordization" and mechanization of factories and business methods. He and his competitor in the round-the-world race were selected from a group of several hundred applicants which included, to the horror of old-fashioned Japanese, several women. The women were not encouraged, however, and to Araki and Matsui fell the honor of carrying Japan's good-will message around the world. Matsui should reach New York about May 6 westbound to connect with a steamer to Yokohama.

NY Times article April 19, 1928.

47

I was one year old and have no recollections of this event, but according to the newspaper articles unearthed in the National Library in Tokyo by a friend seventy-four years later, I "ran about excitedly babbling at people coming and going." Some articles with photos showed me sitting on my father's lap or in my mother's arms.[5]

My father mobilized his staff at his institute into a planning committee. He was going to test the scientific management he was teaching daily. According to his book, *Around the World in 33 Days*, he divided twelve people into five groups: the Pacific, the U.S., the Atlantic; Europe, and Siberia. One person was selected to be the "Time Adjustment Coordinator" so that the time zones would not be overlooked. Each group was assigned to make the most efficient transportation schedule in their assigned area and present it to the Time Coordinator for further scrutiny of time changes. He printed one thousand timetable cards, on which all pertinent information was to be written for each leg of the trip. On the walls of the planning office were posted the maps of each of the five regions of the world.

Everyone was so focused that sometimes they forgot to eat or sleep, but after ten days of unimaginable effort, they had reduced the time to thirty-three days, twenty hours, thirty-three minutes, and nineteen seconds. The teams felt that this was the very best, believing they could not reduce the time by another minute. In spite of meticulous planning and second and third contingency plans, the *Around the World Race* was not all smooth sailing. The weather hampered the progress of air travel, still in its infancy, and of the ocean voyages both in the Pacific and the Atlantic. There were many hair-raising close calls.

On the other hand, there were some memorable moments, such as when Mrs. Landis, the woman mayor of Seattle, personally welcomed my father. On the *Aquitania*, Miss Helen Wills, the world tennis champion on her way to Wimbledon, spoke to him. His heart was filled with nostalgia when he flew over Ohio, the home of his alma mater.

---

5   The newspaper's name is [*Jiji Shimpo*], April 6, 1928. Japanese newspapers do not credit writers. *Jiji Shimpo* was a major newspaper of that time and followed daily the "around the world" event. My friend in Japan copied ninety-three issues of this event at the National Library in Tokyo and sent them to me.

When he flew into New York City on a mail plane, Mr. James Walker, then mayor of New York, wrote on my father's card:

Greetings and Salutations to All Japan, which I sincerely hope will be conveyed by that "Prince of the Air" Toichiro Araki at the consummation of his trip around-the-world flight.

James Walker, Mayor, New York City

I did some research on my father's trip at the local library (in Brookline, Massachusetts) to see what kind of publicity he'd received outside Japan. I went over the 1928 *New York Times* tape. You can imagine my surprise and joy when I zeroed in on April 19, 1928, the date my father had arrived in New York, to find a substantial coverage on my father's landing. The headline and story read:

JAPANESE ARRIVES ON WORLD RACE EAST.

After Brief Stay He Sails on Aquitania, Expecting to Cross Rival Near London. Left Tokio (sic) 12 Days ago. He Shows Efficiency in Shaving, Greeting Compatriots and Being Interviewed. ASKS PUBLIC TO WRITE HIM And Tell the Difference Between Buddhism and Christianity and How Dry We Are. Toichiro Araki, a 34-year old Japanese businessman, who is the east-bound contestant in a two-man race in opposite directions around the world from Tokio (sic), dropped into New York in a mail plane from San Francisco via Cleveland, yesterday afternoon half an hour ahead of his schedule.*

In *Around the World in 33 Days*, my father wrote of his arrival in New York City:

Reporters, cameramen and welcoming ladies suddenly appeared from nowhere and surrounded me. I had not slept for a day and a half, and my face was unshaven and looked tired. "I don't want to show such a dirty face to the citizens of America. Please wait until I shave," I begged. Good-naturedly nonchalant Americans said, the unshaven, tired face is what makes good news, but finally relented and allowed me to shave and freshen up. While I was shaving in the corner of the hangar, a group of young women came to watch me. I didn't mind getting publicity for my trip, but I was at a loss to what to do with a chatty group of young women who gathered around me. So I said, politely, "I respect good manners as much as you do. I've been told that American young ladies do not watch a strange man shave," and they finally left me alone.

What touched me the most when I read about his race around the world was that he remained calm, even at the most hair-raising moments, and his audacity and charm would draw total strangers into his support. That was the essence of my father—a man of extraordinary charisma and charm.

He won the race—in thirty-three days, sixteen hours, thirty-three minutes, and twenty-nine seconds—yes, that is what made this event so newsworthy—and received a national hero's welcome. Just as my mother had predicted, his business took off and planted a seed of the concept of "efficiency" in Japanese consciousness.

CHAPTER V: BALANCING EAST AND WEST

Tokyo in the 1930s

My sisters and I lived a fairly carefree and privileged life growing up in Hatsudai, a bucolic suburb of Tokyo in the 1930s. We lived in a big house that had a backyard with a small swimming pool, unheard of in those days, except for movie stars. My father was very fussy when it came to the health of his children and feared we may catch disease in the town swimming pool. Seeing the unbelievable congestion of today, it is hard to imagine, but in the 1930s, Tokyo was spotted with fields and woods and even a small dairy farm near our house, where a young man on bicycle delivered milk in small, glass bottles to our home early in the morning.

It was a time when Japan was still steeped in the ancient tradition of class division—between the samurai and the commoner. Below our names, our elementary school graduation certificates listed whether the student was from the samurai class or the commoner. Intermarriage of the two classes was frowned upon. This class division was broken with the introduction of American democracy after Japan was defeated in the Pacific War in 1945.

Me, Tarzan!

With so little contact with boys in my life and little exposure to adult life in the pre-TV era, I naively hoped and believed that I'd grow up to be a boy. I did "boy things," such as climbing trees or being Tarzan when we played. Johnny Weismueller's jungle yell had reached Japan and stirred every child's heart. My elder sister played Jane and our youngest sister, the baby. I would hang a rope around the Ginko tree in our backyard, give my jungle yell, and swing from it. Or I would wrestle with an imaginary beast to protect "my family." When rain kept us from going outside to play, we would turn the dining room chairs upside down to make them look as if they were big rocks, and we would take shelter under the dining room table. While "Jane" looked after "the baby," I went to hunt for food and encountered many ferocious animals. My mother never objected, so long as we were not endangering ourselves. Of course when mealtimes arrived, we had to return to the real world.

Morphing into a Ballerina

When I was in seventh grade, my mother finally enrolled me in a ballet school, hoping that I would learn a bit of grace. Exposure to ballet opened a new world for me. I was smitten with the beauty of ballet and imagined that I would someday become a ballerina. Sadly, I discovered that I did not have the talent, and preparation for my college entrance examination preempted my dance lessons as the war progressed rapidly.

My Father's Influence

Efficiency and pragmatism were what we girls learned from our father. He also generously gave his time to teach us many other things. This was unusual in a Japanese home, where father was a distant figure and was seldom at home. My father was truly a hands-on father, who changed our diapers and fed us when we were babies. He attended PTA meetings and became the talk of the school. "What a wonderful father you have!" my classmates would exclaim with envy.

In his book, *Dream Journey*, about his student days in America from 1918 to 1921, he wrote that one of the things that impressed him was the shapely legs of American women. Most Japanese homes in those days had Tatami mat rooms where people sat on the floor with their legs tucked under, and it was common to see Japanese women with squatty legs referred to as *daikon ashi* (daikon-shaped leg). Daikon is a long, round, white radish, a favorite Japanese food. He promised himself that, if he had daughters, they would not sit on the floor and get daikon ashi. So he designed our nursery in a completely western style, with beds, desks, and chairs. Our living room and dining room were also western style, so we never sat on the floor to study or eat meals.

When we were very young, my father had a large sand box and a tiny wading pool built in our backyard, and as we grew older, he took over my mother's flower garden and designed a bigger swimming pool, just wide enough and deep enough—about twelve feet by six feet wide and four feet deep with wide steps on either end—for us to safely enjoy endless summer afternoons. No one imagined that, a decade later, the pool would be converted into a perfect air-raid shelter and protect us from firebombing.

While we were still in grammar school, my father taught us how to play poker and bridge. He also taught us ballroom dancing, which he learned while he was a student in the United States. At Christmas time, my elder sister and I, in white French-lace dresses my mother designed and made, would accompany our parents to the Rotary Club family party at Teikoku Hotel (Imperial Hotel) and waltz and Foxtrot amid the foreigners' exclamations of, "Oh-how cute!" or "How sweet!" We grew up unafraid of seeing tall white people with blue eyes who were very different from us and hearing a language that was not Japanese.

We watched with adoration our parents glide and twirl in the living room where the carpet was rolled up in corner and chairs + table were pushed against the wall...

narrow and high Zori.

felt sole for easy gliding.

half stocking, white.

Tabi: footwear

Special Zōri (footwear), modesty half leg cover, and Tabi (footwear) for Dancing in Kimonos.

When we were in grade school, my father would play on the piano and teach us an American song called, "Row, Row, Row Your Boat." We liked the merry tune. The *r* and *th* sounds that are nonexistent in

Japanese were difficult for us, and the words came out, "Lo, lo, lo ya bot, jentolee down za sutoleem. Mehly, mehly mehly, mehly, life is butta doleem!"

At home, efficiency was first and foremost in every phase of our lives. Although he did not use a stopwatch, as Mr. Gilbreth of *Cheaper by the Dozen* fame had done, my father constantly admonished us, "Don't waste time! Think ahead, plan, and do one thing while doing something else. Don't let your head and hands be idle." When buttoning a blouse, "Start with the bottom button," he would tell us, "to avoid misalignment and having to start all over—a waste of time!"

Balancing East and West: High Brow and Low Brow

Our life was truly "*Wayoh Secchu*" (a mixture of East and West). The children's room, living room, and dining room were western style with parquet floors, tables, and chairs, but my parents' room, guest's room, and the maid's room were Japanese, with tatami mats. My father went to work in business suits, but as soon as he returned home, he would change into kimono. My mother wore a kimono in the winter and a dress in the summer, but when she went out, she usually wore a kimono. We wore dresses or school uniforms most of the time. On New Year's Day, the most important holiday in Japan, or on other special occasions, we wore formal kimonos. Meals too were a mixture of East and West.

Even entertainment ran the gamut of Japanese to Occidental and highbrow to lowbrow. Our parents introduced us to Kabuki, the Japanese traditional theater, and Bunraku, the ancient puppetry, as well as opera and ballet. But I think my father's favorite was Yoseh, the Japanese vaudeville. Mother was not too keen on the idea of us going to vaudeville and never accompanied us, but my father insisted that *real* Japanese life was experienced at Yoseh. Father called it "going to school."

On some Saturday nights, while we were playing in our room upstairs, we'd hear, "Hey, kids, let's go to school!" The words would be music to our ears. We dropped whatever we were doing and ran downstairs to go to "school."

Yoseh was like an old Japanese theater where you checked your shoes at the entrance, and sat on the floor to watch "sit-down comedy" (as opposed to Western stand-up comic), acrobats, singing, and dancing.

Yoseh was a small theatre and the audience section had tatami mat floors, where we sat with our legs tucked under. We went upstairs to a box where servers gave us cushions to sit on and some green tea. A woman came around selling tangerines and sweet bean cakes. We didn't always understand the humor, but we loved being with a lively crowd in an "exotic" atmosphere. When we told our friends at school that we went to Yoseh, many didn't even know what that was, and those who knew raised their eyebrows in disapproval.

Yoseh
(Japanese Vaudeville)

My father believed in well-rounded education for us from high brow to low brow. -- Opera to vaudeville.

Hollywood movies were extremely popular in prewar Japan. We played with Shirley Temple paper dolls, and we would make different outfits for her of our own creation. Being a tomboy, I was particularly fond of Johnny Weissmuller in *Tarzan*, and we often played "Jungle." When we were in our teens, we never missed Deanna Durbin's movies. We collected photos of Hollywood movie stars with their "signatures" like boys collected baseball cards.

Women's Education in Prewar Japan

My dream of going to America to study like my father had done continued to drive me. I set my goal of entering Tsuda Eigaku Juku (now called Tsuda Juku College), a premier women's college considered the top English education college in Japan and the sister college of Bryn Mawr College (University today) in Connecticut. In 1941 and 1942, my last two years in high school, it became my consuming goal to put my energy into passing the test to enter Tsuda Juku, founded in 1900 by Umeko Tsuda, a pioneer in women's education who had graduated from Bryn Mawr. The school was known for its rigorous academic program and seemed to draw iconoclastic and independent women. In the pre-World War II Japan, women were not allowed to attend the then all-male universities such as Tokyo, Keio, and Waseda. Women did not yet have voting rights.

After graduation, the majority of my high school classmates married through traditional arrangements called *omiai*, made by go-betweens. In 1943, out of my graduating class of eighty, only a handful went to college, and the rest eagerly engaged in learning literature, flower arrangement, tea ceremony, sewing and cooking—prerequisites to being a good homemaker.

Miss Trott and Mrs. Kirkham

Lady Luck smiled upon me when I was in seventh grade, in 1940. Daily English class was introduced in our curriculum. Our English teachers, Miss Trott and Mrs. Kirkham, were both British, but they were a world apart in appearance and lifestyle. Miss Trott, a large, rotund middle-aged woman with pale gray eyes and gray hair tied tightly in a bun in the back, wore glasses and comfortable shoes. Young and pretty Mrs. Kirkham had wavy, golden hair and deep blue eyes and dressed smartly in suits. All the girls were crazy about Mrs. Kirkham and treated her with adoration, as if she were a movie star. In girls' schools, the objects of adolescent passion were other females in school in a platonic, puppy love kind of way, which we grew out of when we found the opposite gender.

In the fall of 1943, I took a three-day grueling entrance examination at Tsuda Eigakujuku. I also applied to two other "safe" colleges in case I was not accepted at Tsuda. I don't recall exactly what day or month in early 1944 a letter arrived from Tsuda, but I do recall with such clarity what I did and said at that moment. I was afraid to open the envelope in front of my family, so I went into the bathroom, locked the door, and with trembling hands, slowly opened the envelope.

"Dear Miss Araki, We are happy to inform you ..."

I burst out of the bathroom whooping and yelling. I ran around the house with the letter held high above my head saying, "I got in! I got in!"

Everyone shouted, *"Omedetou! Omedetou!* (Congratulations)."

I felt as if I were on top of the world. Without my realizing it at the time, this was a defining moment in my life. A chain of events that happened while I was a student at Tsuda would lead me to a path I had never imagined.

CHAPTER VI: GOOD-BYE, JAPAN; HELLO, AMERICA

Farewell to Juuko-san

In 1948, President Truman passed another decree—all servicemen who married Japanese women must return to the States with their wives by the end of 1948. Many farewell parties were hurriedly planned.

While Earl and I were busily preparing for our departure, a long lost friend, Juuko, unexpectedly showed up at our house. He was a young artist among our friends who used to gather at our tea house for an afternoon of haiku. He had a butch haircut and shy, doe-like eyes. He always wore a dark cotton kimono, as if he were from another era.

When Juuko was in the army, he was so slow and inept that he used to incur the wrath of his superior officers. From what I heard, the Japanese army was no place for the fainthearted. Juuko used to get slapped around a lot. One day, his superior officer punched him so hard that his jaw was broken. He left the army with disability. His jaw was slightly crooked, he could not close his mouth properly, and he spoke with a bit of slur. Whenever he laughed or we took pictures, he would put his hand over his mouth to hide his "shameful" past.

My mother had a habit of collecting the unfortunate and downtrodden. She was particularly touched by Juuko's sweet and kind nature, and he had been included in our haiku group. As the war progressed, young men went off to war, and bombings of Tokyo intensified. Such leisurely pastimes as haiku parties had disappeared from our life, and we'd lost contact with each other.

I was happy but distressed to see Juuko so thin and more shabbily dressed than before.

"Juuko-san! It's good to see you! How have you been?" I asked.

He shyly looked down at his feet and mumbled,

"I heard that you got married and are leaving for America ... I came to say good-bye."

"So, how are you?" I asked. "Where do you live now?"

"My house was bombed, and I lost everything."

"Oh no!" I gasped. "I'm so sorry." I saw the tears well up in his eyes. I took his bony hands in mine and squeezed them.

He lifted his eyes for a second, full of sorrow and said, "I have something I want to give you. It's really a shabby present, but I put my heart into it." He handed me a rectangular package wrapped in old newspaper and tied with a brown string.

"I don't want you to open it now until you arrive in your new home in America."

"Oh, Juuko-san, whatever it is, I know I will love it. Thank you so much!"

After he left, curiosity got the better of me, and I slowly opened the package. Inside was a painting of Mt. Asama, the volcano that had been a catalyst for our poetic gatherings at our summer home. It was painted on a wooden board in a crudely homemade frame. On the back, he had written:

Dearest Madam Nobuko, my dear friend of Oiwake:

I have lost my house and all of my art supplies in the firebombing. This is the painting of our beloved "fire mountain" on my homemade wooden canvas and frame. If this could comfort you even a little in a faraway land called America, I would be so happy. I have lost over two thousand books, and I'm so poor now, but saying good-bye to you is saddest of all. But we cannot fight destiny. I hope and pray for your happiness. I shall never forget those happy summer days in Oiwake when we picked mulberries together.

Juuko Iwamitsu

I cried out, so touched by his love and kindness.

The *Fire Mountain* did follow me to Illinois and to Boston. After six decades, and many moves, the handmade frame is gone, but Mt. Asama, puffing out a wispy smoke above tiny brown farmhouses dotted in the green fields and woods, sits on my desk as a memento of the age of innocence so long ago.

Good-bye, Japan

On October 8, 1948, we sailed from Yokohama on an army transport ship for a transpacific voyage headed for Seattle. The early morning sky was gray as we gathered at our gate for our final family photo. Father was in a dark suit with an open collar shirt (he hated ties). My mother in kimono; elder sister, Keiko, and her three-year old daughter, Sumiko; and my younger sister, Aiko, stood beside Earle and me. My blue suit mother made for me amply covered my five-month-pregnant belly.

We all had somber expressions. On everyone's mind was one question: *Will we ever see each other again?* It was decades before commercial jets would carry millions around the globe or talking on the telephone overseas would become like talking to your neighbor.

My mother, so grief-stricken by the impending separation, did not accompany me to the wharf, but my relatives and friends gathered to see us off. Tearful farewells—"Take care," "Stay healthy," "Don't forget to write!" "Please come back!"—were repeated over and over again. Occasionally someone jokingly said, "We'll come and see you some day!" Those words seemed like a pipe dream and made us laugh. After we boarded, we leaned over the railing as far as possible to get a better look at the crowd below waving their hands and handkerchiefs.

We felt the rumbling of the engines start through the deck under our feet. The deafening blast of the ship's horn made everyone jump. "Good-bye! Good-bye, Japan!"

The tears blurred everyone. *I may never see my country again.* Suddenly, I was filled with remorse for my reckless and audacious act. This is not what I'd had in mind when I'd dreamed of going to America. I was to go to America to study and come back, not to live there forever! The ship slowly left the wharf, and I saw my classmate, Yuri, who was eight months pregnant, run to the tip of the wharf, waving her hand. She stood there until we could no longer see each other.

This was no luxury ocean liner; the accommodations were Spartan but tolerable.

With rows of bunk beds, there was no privacy. Men and women were separated. This was an army ship, and Earle and I had cabins on different decks. We did eat together in the dining hall. In the game room, we played chess, and on the deck, shuffleboard, and I learned to play bingo and even won a radio. The October sea was cold and unfriendly, and the eleven days on the Pacific seemed like eternity.

Sometimes I watched the waves the ship left behind and consoled myself that this sea was connected to Japan. Some of my friends had said that I would not last even three years in America.

I'll show them, I vowed. *I'll be strong and will not be defeated.*

Hello, America!

After eleven days on the sea, we arrived in Seattle in mid-October. Seattle had many Japanese immigrants who had left the hard life of farmers decades before to seek a better life in America. The men and women had built a "Japan town," with restaurants and shops that made them think of home. To my delight, Earle, who sensed that I might already be missing Japanese food, took me to a Japanese restaurant.

I bought a bunch of bananas and devoured them all at our hotel while Earle watched, bemused. He couldn't imagine not having bananas for three years! We hadn't had fresh bananas for the duration of the war because the seas between Japan and Formosa where the bananas came from were battlefields. I was a little encouraged that one could find Japanese food and to see that other Japanese immigrants had succeeded in adapting to the new culture.

After two days in Seattle, we boarded a Pullman train to Chicago. The three days of crossing America from the West Coast to the heartland is only a blur in my memory. The only thing that stayed in my mind was the vastness of this country—miles upon miles upon miles of wheat fields, grasslands, mountains, forests, rivers, and desert, only broken occasionally by cities and towns. The contrast to the miniature garden-like topography of Japan was awesome. In land space, America is twenty-five times larger than Japan; yet, the American population is only twice that of Japan.

In the dining car, everyone dressed up, and I wore my black silk dress with a pink floral pattern, which my mother had made for me, and the black pearl necklace and earrings she'd given me as a parting gift, which received a lot of compliments. Sadly, I was to discover later, when I opened my suitcase in our new home, that my black pearl necklace and earrings had disappeared. That did not bode well with me, as I came from a country that used to boast that 90 percent of articles left on buses, trains, and taxis were returned to their rightful owners.

After the third day of traveling, we arrived in Chicago and changed to a local train headed south for Champaign, where Earle's family lived. Around 7:00 p.m., we arrived in Champaign, a small country station then. The October night was dark and cold. Only a few people got off. I looked around to see if any of Earle's family was waiting for us. Earle had been overseas for three years. The station was deserted. I went to the ladies' room to make myself presentable to my new family, whom I was to meet soon. Under the dim light in an old, dingy station bathroom, looking in the smudged mirror, I was filled with a sense of foreboding.

We took a taxi to Earle's home.

First meeting with my in-laws

The first one to answer the doorbell was Earle's eight-year-old sister, Connie. I had seen her in photos and recognized her.

"How do you do! You must be Connie," I called out. "Hi!"

Connie answered cheerfully with a big smile.

Earle said, "Hi, sis!" and gave her a big hug.

Then mother appeared at the door and filled with gladness, cried out, "Earle!" She embraced the son she hadn't seen in three years.

The family welcomed Earle with hugs and kisses, which was an alien custom to me. Everyone seemed a little nervous and treated me gingerly, not knowing exactly what to expect.

They all spoke at once: "Come in, come in, meet everybody!" "You must be exhausted!" "How was the trip?"

As we walked into the large living room, Earl's family showered us with chatter. His older sister, Berniece, who had curly, brown hair and a chubby face and was a coed at the University of Illinois, and his pretty high school majorette sister, Claudine, came running down the stairs. While Earle hugged his sisters and shook hands with his father, I shook hands with everybody and said a polite "How do you do."

A few minutes later, a tall, slightly stooped elderly man appeared from nowhere. I learned he was Earle's eighty-year-old-grandfather, who lived in the basement.

We heard footsteps from upstairs, and Earle's big brother, Hal, a tall graduate student at the University of Illinois with a big smile, and his pretty, pregnant wife, Jan, came down from their second-floor apartment and joined us. More greetings—"Hi, brother. Good to see you! Welcome home!"—ensued.

While Earle related to his family our ocean voyage and the train crossing of the continent, everyone politely watched me. I wore blue suit my mother had made me, which hid my five-month pregnant belly. I saw Claudine watch me intently and whisper something into her mother's ear.

Mother saw my worried look, and to dispel any suspicion, said to me, "Claudine says you don't look pregnant because you are so slim."

I smiled and nodded, not knowing what I should say. This silent smiling became my first line of defense for some time until I mastered English.

We were familiar with each other through exchange of many photographs, and Earle's family seemed relieved that I was able to speak English, albeit haltingly. Eight members of his family lived under one roof. Earle's father was a foreman at Johns Manville Floor Tile Company and his mother, a full-time homemaker. The three-storied house was huge by Japanese standards. Situated on a quiet, residential street, it was white, just as I had seen long ago in photos that had fueled my dreams of going to America, but it had no white picket fence. Earle and I occupied two rooms on the second floor, next to the two rooms with a kitchenette occupied by his brother and his wife. His three sisters occupied the third-floor rooms, and his parents' bedroom was on the first floor off of the dining room. Grandpa lived in the basement.

Until a small kitchenette was installed in one of our two rooms, Earle and I ate our meals with the rest of the family. I was introduced to cottage cheese, ham hocks and navy beans, and beef liver, all of which seemed like horrible food to me at the time, but which I grew to tolerate.

Depth of Cultural Divide

The home of the University of Illinois, 1948 Champaign, was a small, quiet college town about one hundred miles south of Chicago. Church Street where we lived was a wide avenue leading out of the center of the town lined with majestic elm trees. Two or three-storied attractive brick homes and white, shingled homes with well-tended, inviting lawns in front lined the street.

People sat on porch swings and watched the goings-on in the street or said "hi" to the passing neighbors. This was very unusual to me, as in my native country the houses were nearly all enclosed inside tall fences and not at all inviting to passersby. The manicured gardens and lawns were hidden from public eye, only for the enjoyment of the occupants. Soon I learned to love this leisurely American custom and joined my in-laws in their neighborhood gossip.

A bus stopped across the street from our house and took us into downtown—a modest collection of churches, Piggly Wiggly and Kroger's grocery stores, a couple of movie theaters, a furniture store, a few clothing stores, a five-and-dime store, and the ubiquitous Walgreen's, none of them more than two stories high.

A cultural divide popped up even in small daily affairs. Whenever I poured a cup of coffee for my new husband, he would look at it, and say, "Hey, you only gave me half a cup."

I would look into the cup and see that it was just "the right" amount. In Japan, one never filled a cup or a plate to the brim. We were taught to fill it three-fourths. Filling drinks or plates to the brim was considered gauche. This custom was a natural outgrowth of understatement in all things Japanese. On the other hand, when my husband gave me a cup of tea, he would fill it to the brim, and instantly, the sight of such fullness took my appetite away, and I had to pour a portion of it in the sink before I would want to drink it. What a cultural chasm existed between the land of plenty and the land of poor!

Mother's First Letter

In 1948, international postal service was nothing like what it is today. If we were lucky, airmail letters arrived in two weeks. My mother wrote her first letter to me on October 18, ten days after I had left Japan; it arrived in Champaign on November 1—the very first letter from Japan! I curled up on the bed alone and, with my heart racing, opened it carefully, making sure that no part was torn.

Dear Nobuko-chan,

I hope your ocean voyage was smooth and uneventful. I thought of going to the wharf to see you one more time, but your father and sisters advised against it as I was so distraught.

66

Your friends came back to our house and reported to me in detail how the departure went. It's been ten days but it seems as if it was yesterday. Maybe five years would go by quickly and you'll be back in no time. I think of the day of your return, and now I don't cry so much. But whenever I go into your empty house and see some things that you left behind, I start to cry. I hung your small photo, with a pressed four-leaf clover you found, above my desk, and whenever I feel tired, I look at it and am comforted.

I hope you were not too seasick. Until I receive your letter, I cannot stop worrying. I'm sure there are things that are far better there than in Japan, but there is nothing like your own country that gives you sustenance. The quickest way to your happiness is to become adjusted to your host country. Cooperate and learn from everyone.

Tell me all about "Bunny's" family. Knowing him, I feel confident that his family are good people. Even if you encounter some unpleasantness, do not be discouraged. Don't blame "Bunny." Try to get along. Please write everything in detail about your new life in your adopted country. We are all anxiously waiting to hear from you.

During the day I am busy attending to various things and distracted, but when the evening comes, especially at a mealtime when we have your favorite food, I start to cry thinking how much you would love it, and am scolded by your father and sisters for being so maudlin, so I'm trying very hard to be strong and stoic. You must miss Japanese food!

You may be so exhausted from the long trip and becoming acquainted with your new environment that you may not feel like writing for a while, but as soon as you get your strength back, write to me about the life of the Barcus family from the morning to night without skipping anything.

Your little three-year old niece, Sumiko, surprised us by saying, "When I grow up I'm going to America to see aunt

Nobuko, so grandma, will you give me some money?" The farewell photo we took on the day of your departure is enclosed. There is a strange story about this photo.

The day after the photo was delivered to our house, we had a power outage. We were eating our dinner with candlelight. The doorbell rang and we found a middle-aged woman accompanied by an employee of the photo studio who had taken our pictures. When we inquired what the purpose of their visit was, the middle-aged woman said her lost daughter was living here! She said she saw her in the photo. So I brought our family farewell photo and showed it to her, and she said, "Yes! This is my daughter!" pointing to you, and asked me how I came to know her lost daughter. We were dumbfounded and lost for words. I told her that this was my second daughter who left for America only recently. She kept asking, "Really? Really she is your daughter?" Then she told me two years ago, her daughter who looked just like you ran away with an American soldier. She saw our farewell photo at the studio and thought she had finally found her lost daughter. She kept looking at the photo with candlelight, unconvinced that it was not her daughter. I felt so sorry for this woman, so I brought out other photos of you, and she was finally convinced and left.

Christmas is near. Please let me know which of the gifts you took to your new family were most well received. Did everything arrive safely? I am confident that you are the kind of person who could endure any kind of hardships, and I hope and pray for your happiness. I cannot do anything for you from so far away. The only things I can send you are my prayers and dreams.

Your loving mother

When I finished reading her letter, I could feel her love envelop me and give me strength. I thanked our good fortune that I was not her "lost" daughter, but just far away in another land. I read again and again her words, "The quickest way to your happiness is to become adjusted to your host country. Cooperate and learn from everyone." I promised myself that I would.

In 1948, a transpacific phone call not only cost a fortune, but was like talking into an echo chamber, having to repeat over and over again, "Can you hear me? Can you hear me?" And sometimes the call would be lost altogether. The overseas phone was something one would use only in dire emergency, such as when someone died. Letters were our lifeline. So it was understandable that my mother worried about me in the "new" country. She wrote on November 19, 1948, forty-two days after I'd left Japan:

Dear Nobuko chan,

Received your first letter on November 7. We were all simply overjoyed to know the detailed accounts of your trip across the Pacific. We could almost see what kind of town Seattle is. It sounds as if some Japanese food is available there, so you may not feel so homesick ... We are anxiously waiting to learn all about your life in Champaign. I pray every day for your happiness. That is all I can do for you now. I suppose every mother worries about her children when they are far away and imagine the worst ... What were you doing on November 11? I had a strange dream just after I fell asleep. They say the early evening dreams are just the opposite of what will happen, so maybe I shouldn't worry, but I was overcome with melancholy. Your elder sister Keiko said she, too, had a bad dream. So now, I'm worried sick. On the night of the 11th, I felt a cold coming on, so I went to bed early.

My dream: I was sewing something on my Singer sewing machine and felt a presence in the room, so I turned around, and you were sitting there in your navy blue slacks. I went over and took your hand and said, "Nobuko -chan, what happened?" You just smiled and would not answer. I kept shaking your hand and kept asking, "What happened? What happened?" Then you finally told me that "Bunny found a new girlfriend on the ship and took her back to his home, so I came back." I was so shocked that I could hardly breathe. I held you in my arms and

69

started to bawl, saying, "I never thought Bunny would do such a thing! Why are you so weak?" My crying out loud woke me.

Your elder sister Keiko's dream was that she saw you sitting in the patio in an old dirty jacket, and you told her that you came home because Bunny and his mother scolded you every day, and you couldn't take it anymore. It's probably because I'm thinking about you so much every day that my imagination is getting the best of me. I am sure that kind and gentle Bunny is even more attentive than ever and is taking good care of you who entrusted your life to him leaving your family and country … If you have any unhappy feelings, don't keep it to yourself. Write to me. I know I would worry, but I would know how you'd overcome difficult situations and feel more and more confident of your ability to survive. We are going to bed early tonight as Hurricane Agnes is expected.

Bunny's good legacy still lingers. Whenever relatives and friends talk about Bunny, we are all filled with such warm and loving thoughts of that sweet and fun-loving boy. Please translate this to Bunny: "Bunny-san, how are you? Please remember the Japanese words you learned." Please take good care of your health.

Mother

I replied bravely, "Don't worry, no such thing will happen! Everyone is kind to me." I did not mention how nervous and tense I was all day in a totally foreign environment and how I kept it to myself because I did not want to worry Earle and spent many sleepless nights. I tucked away her admonition, "Why are you so weak?" deep in my heart, and resolved to be strong.

In response to my letter describing the life in America, mother wrote me:

Dearest Nobuko chan,

We were so happy and relieved to receive your letter detailing your life in America. Everything you tell us is so fascinating that we take turns reading it aloud at dinner. Sometimes, as we read along, we start to cry with joy when you tell us how kind and caring your in-laws are to you. I'm sure not everything is great, and you may encounter many hardships in the future, but I feel confident that you'll not make the same mistake your elder sister made. [She was talking about my sister's divorce.]

Japan is still recovering from the war and goods are scarce, but we do want to send you and your new family something for Christmas. I'm sending a tablecloth and napkin set for your mother-in-law, compacts for your older sisters-in-law, for your younger sister-in-law a silk tie-dyed scarf, for your youngest sister-in-law a pair of Japanese wooden clogs with bells inside. They are not practical, but I thought they are cute and fun. I don't know what to send to menfolk, so I decided not to send anything at all. I'm sure in a year or two, Japan will have things that can be sent abroad without shame. I hope everyone will understand.

I pray every day that your life in America is a happy one. With all of us here praying for you, how could it be otherwise? We are envious of the central heating American homes have, and we drooled over the delicious cake you told us about. We could feel the loving environment "Bunny's" family is providing for you. Your father is very pleased.

Mother

I could picture my family at the dinner table reading my letter, laughing and crying and trying to imagine what my life in America was like. I was touched by my mother's thoughtfulness, that she would send Christmas presents to my new American family when Tokyo was still recovering from the devastation of the war.

My First Halloween and Football

Within a week after my arrival, I encountered a strange American custom: Children in masquerade were going from door to door in their neighborhoods begging for candies, and if they received no candies, they would play a trick on their neighbors! Earle's youngest eight-year-old sister was dressed as Cinderella. At the end of the evening, she showed me her bag full of candies of all kinds and shared some with

71

me. When my children were old enough to go trick-or-treating, we spent considerable time and energy in making up the most creative costumes, and sometimes the candies turned up under the sofa cushions and behind bookcases months later. I'm glad that I was able to experience the time of innocence in America when children freely roamed the streets without fear.

But such time of innocence was also a time of ignorance. "Diversity" was not yet in American consciousness in 1948. The immigrants were told, "When in Rome, do as the Romans do." The Americanization of immigrants was paramount. The accepted thinking was that, if I wanted to speak Japanese, eat Japanese food and do Japanese things, I should stay in Japan. When you are in America, you'll learn to speak English and do things the American way. *The sooner I learn the American way, the faster I'll be accepted as a full-fledged member of the society.* This was the message I got. My own mother encouraged the same. Bilingual education was not yet in the American vocabulary.

Another American experience I encountered within a week of my arrival in the new country was high school football. Earle's pretty younger sister, Claudine, was a popular majorette who had a boyfriend on the football team. The family piled into Dad's and Hal's cars and went to cheer the Champaign High team, the Maroons. I had seen men's college rugby matches and ice hockey games in Japan, but I had never seen anything quite like this raucous football game in my life. The band in their dazzling uniforms, following high-stepping Claudine who beamed a radiant smile as she twirled her baton, marched on to the field, and cheers went up. Earle tried to explain to me what the game was all about, but most of the words were not yet in my vocabulary, and I had no idea what those boys were trying to do.

The bang and crash of the six-foot linesmen and the thunderous roars from the bleachers were astonishing to me. Mothers, fathers, brothers and sisters, even uncles and cousins of every player seemed to be in the bleachers cheering on their favorites. Whenever people stood up and yelled, "Yeah, team!" or whatever they were saying, I joined in and yelled.

I never dreamed that twenty years later, I would be shouting and cheering my son, a celebrated running back at the Brookline High School football games, and fifty years later, I'd again be cheering, this time for my grandson, Dorian, a quarterback for the Boston Latin Academy. Nor would I have guessed that I would become an ardent fan of the New England Patriots.

My First Thanksgiving

Having a Japanese war bride in the small college town of Champaign only three years after the end of the war was news. A photo of Earle and me appeared in the *Gazette* during the week of my first Thanksgiving in America.

I watched in wonderment as my mother-in-law stuffed a twenty-pound turkey; made giblet gravy, mashed potatoes, and heavenly stuffing; and baked several kinds of pies. I helped to make mashed potatoes with a masher.

Just as we were getting ready to sit down for a feast, the phone rang. A woman who saw our photo in the paper had called Mother to express her "condolences" for having to live with a "Jap." Mother calmly told the anonymous caller, "We are happy to have a new daughter-in-law from Japan." She may or may not have loved me, but her love for her son was unconditional, and she accepted me as a part of her son's life. I'm truly indebted to this wonderful woman.

"Mother"

Earle's mother, Edna, was nothing like the American women I had seen in Hollywood movies when I was growing up. She never wore makeup. She dressed in a cotton print housedress with a bib apron over it and a pair of medium-heeled sensible shoes at all times, except on Sundays when she went to church. She was a small woman—about five foot four and around one hundred fifteen pounds, not much bigger than me. She was a transplant from England; her father, a coal miner, had immigrated to Canada then to the United States when she was a little girl. Although she had little formal education, Edna was self-educated, and there was a kind of quiet dignity about her that I liked. I could tell right away that she was the pillar of this family. She was a wise and stoic woman. She reminded me of the traditional Japanese woman, gentle and quiet but with fierce inner strength. The difference was that she had that American independent spirit and strong religious beliefs.

What shocked me was how hard she worked. She not only cleaned the big ten-room house all by herself, she looked after her elderly father-in-law who lived in the basement and a lodger who rented a room on the second floor; did the laundry for the entire family; cooked, shopped, and ironed; mowed the grass with a manual mower; shoveled coal in the furnace; and in her "spare" time, painted walls, sewed her daughters' dresses, and even took in sewing for others. I could tell that Earle not only loved his mother but also had great respect for her. I made up my mind that, if I were to be Earle's good wife, I needed to emulate my mother-in-law. So, I followed her around observing and sometimes helping and learning to cook, clean, and wash the American way.

Since all of her children called Edna "Mother," I, too, called her "Mother." I have never seen my mother work like that. My American mother never asked any of her children to help. She had no maids to help her. I felt so sorry for my mother-in-law that, even after I had my baby and I had enough work, I couldn't help volunteering my assistance to her.

Before the age of polyester, we ironed everything. I even ironed sheets! I often volunteered to iron mother's laundry, which included cotton dresses for Mother and my sisters-in-law. I was meticulous and was especially good at ironing ruffles. Everyone praised me, which spurred me on, and I ironed away with an aching back, regretting when I got in over my head.

My father-in-law worked very hard outside of the home but rarely lifted his hand to help with household chores. The only "duty" he had was on Saturday, once a week, to take the grocery list his wife made to Grab-It-Here grocery store, go to the pub and hang out with the men, and bring back the grocery order filled by the clerk at the store.

I have a vivid memory of Mother and me hanging laundry on the backyard clotheslines in the summer. Those were the days the washing machine had a wringer that rung clothes, and nobody had heard about a dryer. The scene was repeated in the winter in the dark basement. At first, mother declined my help. "Oh, you don't have to do that ..." But I insisted. Pretty soon, I think she felt my sincere wish and would teach me. "Faith, put all the towels on the same line, keeping them together with clothespins like this," she would explain as she showed me.

My mother-in-law never drove. Even after it became fashionable for women to wear slacks in the '60s and the '70s, she did not wear slacks until the very last year of her life. She had impeccable manners, always proper, very British, and pretended not to understand her husband's raunchy jokes. She tolerated her husband's smoking and only allowed beer in the house but no hard liquor.

She told me that she had wanted to be a singer and was told that she had a good voice, but lack of time and money had kept her from achieving her aspiration. She instilled in her children, instead, her love of music, and every one of them pursued some musical path, either professionally or as an important hobby. There was always music in the house. Somebody was playing the piano or clarinet or trombone or singing. I was happy to find the piano, albeit old, so that I could play my beloved Chopin.

"Dad"

Chauncey Barcus, Earle's father, who was bald, of medium height, and had a rounded back and large workman's hands, came from a big family whose men became carpenters and farmers. You didn't see my father-in-law putting his arms around his children in a warm, fatherly fashion because his father never did. He went to work, came home, and watched TV while drinking beer, playing cards with his wife, or reading pulp fiction until his wife urged him to come to bed.

He was not a talker, but he loved to tell jokes. It seemed that this was his mode of communication and of bonding with his children. Jokes are probably the most difficult part of learning another culture, as each culture has its own sense of humor based on centuries of history and events, and what is a joke in one culture may be a non-joke in another.

Chauncey would say at the dinner table, "Why did the dirty chicken cross the road twice? Because he was a dirty double-crosser!"

And everyone would roar, except me.

There seemed to be a lot of these chicken-crossing jokes. This was a "killer" for me, as I was the only one not able to join in their laughter. Even after the joke was explained to me, sometimes it wasn't funny to me. But I was determined to master American humor. I listened to radio, before the TV era—to comedians' sketches on Red Skelton, Bob Hope, and other shows—with a pencil and notepad to write down their jokes and try to figure out why they were funny. It was many years before I felt completely at home in the joke-a-thon in the family.

Another thing that Dad loved was card games. I learned to play Oh Hell—in front of Mother, we said Oh Heck—Seven Up, Canasta, and Pinochle. Until the TV came into our lives in the early '50s, Mother and Dad would often play Seven Up at the kitchen table after supper. Every now and then, their grown children joined in, and it turned into a lively poker game.

Thanks to my father's plebeian education, no one had to explain to me how to play poker. Dad's favorite expression, when someone hesitated to bid or play was, "The devil hates a coward!" Once, I was hesitating, and he said, "The devil hates a coward! Are you yella?" And, then he looked at me and realized what he had just said, and chuckled, "I guess you are." I didn't take offense, as I knew he meant no malice.

Chauncey's family was poor, and he'd had to go to work when he was thirteen years old; I sensed that he resented his own father's inability or lack of ambition to support the large family. Chauncey's father was a Bible salesman for Jehovah's Witnesses. Yet, although he was not the eldest son, Chauncey was the one who'd taken in his father when he had no place to go. I sensed that he had a strong sense of right and wrong.

For many years, Dad worked on the railroad as a brakeman. He was self-educated, but he read the paper, kept up with what was going on in the world, and had strong opinions about many things. He had that certain salt-of-the-earth quality of Midwestern men. He was kind to me in his rough but genuine way. Once I came home crying because some people at the store had called me "Jap" and given me a hateful stare. He held my face between his big rough hands and told me, "Don't pay attention to what people say. Just keep smiling!"

During the Great Depression, Chauncey injured his arm at work, and the family moved to a farm so that they could live off of the land. My mother-in-law, a city girl, learned to milk the cow, make cottage cheese, churn the butter, kill chickens, and do the family wash by hand! The family did not have electricity or running water; instead, they used an outhouse and bathed once a week, on Saturdays, in a washtub—a life that seemed so backward and unimaginable to me. Yet, the questions people asked me after I arrived in Illinois ranged from "Do you have electricity in Japan?" to "Have you ever talked on the phone?" I suppose in the '40s, the Americans in small towns and rural areas thought that the Japanese lived a primitive life in little huts.

Cultural Differences

Cultural differences created challenges too. In Japan, we made polite talk to smooth the atmosphere in conversations. The idea was to create "harmony." Sometimes we said what we really didn't mean, but since the Japanese understood each other, it was literally taken as polite talk and nothing more.

In America, the situation was quite different, I found out. You only said what you meant. I can fully understand now why this is so in a nation of immigrants of all races, nationalities, and religions. Without a common language and culture, you must speak what you mean in order to understand each other. But I was a newcomer, still steeped in Japanese culture.

My "polite talks" got me in trouble sometimes. After dinner, I would offer to do the dishes, fully expecting a Japanese answer of, "Oh, no, you are very kind to offer, but you don't need to!" Instead, I'd receive an American answer, "Oh thanks. Faith offered to do the dishes!" Mother always stayed behind, and we usually did the dishes together.

Our first child was due in mid-February 1949. Carrying the laundry basket to and from our second-floor apartment and the laundry room in the basement had put an extra strain on my back that was already straining from the weight of the unborn child in my frail one hundred-pound body, unaccustomed to heavy work.

When I was seven months pregnant, one day, I climbed the stairs to our apartment with a big wicker basket full of laundry, as I had done many times. I put the basket down and bent over to pick up the towels. Suddenly, a sharp *zing* ran through my spine, and I could not move. Apparently, my back had finally given out, and I was unable to walk. The pain was unbearable. I called out, "Mother! Mother!"

She came running up the stairs and found me paralyzed by the bed. She put me gently on the bed as I gnashed my teeth to keep from screaming. She then brought a heating pad. It never occurred to me to go to a doctor.

The Barcus family did not run to a doctor with every ache and pain of life. We persevered. We had never heard of chiropractors in those days. After a few days, I was finally able to walk from the bedroom to the living room, and for several days, I sat on a couch on an inner tube my mother-in-law had given me to keep the pressure off my spine and a heating pad on my lower back. This was the beginning of a thirty-year battle with my back problem. I wrote my mother:

Dear Mother,

After two weeks of bed rest, my back is healing slowly. I cannot go up and down the stairs yet. "Mother" did our laundry twice already. She is so kind and thoughtful. I don't have to ask her. She just comes around and says, "Isn't it time for laundry?" She must be the best mother-in-law in the world! I am so fortunate! After being cooped up in the house for two weeks, just to get some fresh air, Bunny and his elder sister, Berniece took me out for a slow walk around the block. Although it was freezing cold outside, I think the walk was good for me, and I feel much better. Talk about being cold, you cannot imagine how cold it gets in Illinois. We never have this kind of cold weather in Tokyo! It was 18 degrees below zero! (Centigrade) the other day, and people tell me that it gets colder in February. I don't know if I could survive. I have to wear earmuffs when I go out, otherwise, my ears will fall off!

No Sweet Dependence: Learning to Ask

In Japan, there is a word, *a-ma-e* which loosely translates to "sweet dependence." It is a kind of tacit understanding and expectations that you will be taken care of by the people around you without having to ask. It goes with the Japanese concept of *I-shin Den-shin*—reading your mind. It is a Japanese practice to try to read each other's mind and to meet the other person's needs. In Japanese culture, this is considered true kindness. Such reading of minds is only possible in a totally homogeneous society like Japan where everyone speaks the same language, believes in the same religion, and shares the same values.

Japanese are surprised when they go abroad, and this does not happen; they have to verbally express their needs to others before their needs are met. This *amae* socialization has caused many tragicomedies for Japanese abroad.

I was no exception, although I had been brought up to be more independent-spirited than most Japanese children. This was a hard lesson for me to learn. In old Japan, if someone offered you some food or drink, good etiquette required that you refuse politely first, and only when the person insisted the second and third time, you would politely accept their offering. But in America, if you said "No," the first time, no one insisted the second or third time. I found this out the hard way by going hungry or thirsty when I really wanted some food or drink.

Witch Hazel, Epsom Salt, Mineral Oil, and Vaseline

The Barcus family lived a simple life. Witch hazel, Epsom salt, mineral oil, Vaseline, alcohol, and iodine were what I found in mother's medicine cabinet. Mother taught me to use Witch hazel for insect bites and Epson salts bath for sore muscles or for tired feet. Mother saved my eye once with Vaseline. I was painting the walls of our bedroom and the paint splashed onto my eye. I was a complete novice at painting walls. The Japanese homes had very little wall space, and if there were walls, they were usually unpainted. We never painted the walls ourselves. I ran to Mother for help, and she took a glob of Vaseline and wiped the paint clean off of my eyelid.

Years ago, when Earle's family was living on the farm many miles from a doctor, Mother had to learn to "fix" just about everything without medical help. Once, when he was a boy, Earle almost cut off his thumb while cutting the corn to feed the pigs. His mother washed off the wound, put his dangling thumb back in place, wrapped it with a bandage, and that was that. It's a wonder that he did not die of tetanus. His thumb grew back together, crooked, and with his thumbnail growing in two places. Earle's family simply did not run to a doctor with every cut or pop pills for every pain. They persevered. This is the "medicine" my mother-in-law taught me, which stood me in good stead throughout my parenting days and beyond.

An Honorary "White"?

Bracey, Earle's army buddy and the young man my family "adopted" back in 1946, invited us to his home in Nashville, Tennessee, in December, 1948. After his army stint in Japan, he had returned to his music study at the conservatory. This was my first trip south of the Mason-Dixon Line. Bracey was an only child, and his parents were extremely hospitable people. We went out to dinner at a restaurant and I had to use the restroom. When I got there, for the first time in my life, I saw signs that read: "Whites Only" and "Colored." I knew I was not white, but I wondered if the "colored" meant nonwhite or Negroes. I pondered for a few minutes, returned to the table, and asked Bracey which door I should go into. He laughed and told me that I should use the "Whites Only." I was shocked. I guess Japanese are "honorary White." There were class distinctions in Japan, but nothing as blatantly marked as this.

In Champaign, the local VFW organization had a Christmas party. Earle called to get the tickets to the party and asked, "Can a Japanese national attend the party?"

The answer was, "No."

Looking a little embarrassed Earle told me, "They won't admit Japanese nationals to the party."

The anti-Japanese sentiment was still pretty high. I was not angered or offended by such discrimination, as I believed that only time would heal such feelings. And I was right.

Horseshoes and Croquette

In the summer, on Sundays especially, the family had a backyard barbeque, after which we'd play horseshoes and croquette. The barbeque was an entirely new but fun experience for me, with charcoal broiled hamburgers and hot dogs; sweet, fresh corn on the cob; and giant watermelons, twice the size of watermelons we had in Japan.

What baffled me the most was the game of horseshoes. I could not understand why on earth anybody would want to throw a horseshoe. The menfolk were quite serious about it though. I tried hard to get the rhythm of stepping up and swinging my arm just the right way so that the heavy horseshoe would fly out of my hand making a nice arch and with a *clang* wrap itself around the stake. No matter how hard I tried, I could not coordinate my step and arm, and the horseshoe would fly out of my hand in an unexpected direction far from the stake.

After a while, whenever it was my turn, everyone would say, "Watch out, it's Faith's turn!" and step back out of my reach. After many tries that resulted in total failure, I finally gave up. I think the problem was a general inability to throw things with any accuracy. I tried, but never learned to bowl or throw a softball. There didn't seem to be a good connection between my throwing arm and my brains. But the clanging sound of the horseshoe hitting the stake in the summer night still echoes in my mind with nostalgia.

CHAPTER VII: MOTHERHOOD

Birth of Our Daughter, Julie

Four months had passed since I arrived in Champaign, and I became accustomed to the American way a little by little. But I was not happy with the new culture. The American independent spirit seemed too harsh to me. People's frank talk seemed too rude. I did not develop an affinity for American food. As my belly grew larger, every task became a burden. My back ached. I missed my family and Japan terribly. I missed *amae,* that sweet dependence so unique in Japanese society, where everyone sensed your needs and took care of you without having to ask. I still had not quite mastered the art of expressing in English my thoughts and needs. I smiled a lot, was very agreeable, and everyone, including Earle, thought I was content and happy.

On February 1, I wanted to do something special for Earle's twenty-second birthday. All day, I shopped and cooked, even though my body screamed for rest. Standing at the sink and peeling the shrimp for nearly an hour, I think, may have been the cause—late that night, I began labor; early the next morning, our daughter, Julie, was born, three weeks early.

Mother, I Need You

The labor was not difficult, but it resulted in a considerable tear in the birth canal, which was painful every time I coughed or sneezed. Unlike today, in the 1940s, new mothers were required to stay in bed and not move around. I was so homesick and emotionally drained from the ordeal without the support of my family that I could not even sit up, let alone walk, for a week anyway. The first few days after I returned home until I was able to get back on my feet, Earle's mother slept in the next room so that when the baby woke in the middle of the night, she could bring her to me to nurse. That way, Earle's sleep would not be disturbed, as he had classes to attend in the morning. Today's enlightened belief on childcare and gender roles would surely raise the question: why didn't the child's father get up and help? I don't think such thought ever occurred to us.

The new baby was colicky and cried a lot, probably reflecting my anxiety and depression. I was totally at a loss as to what to do. Most of the time I cried with her, calling out to my mother, "Mother! Mother, I need you!" and sobbing when no one was around. Soon, it was apparent that the reason the baby was crying was because she was not getting enough milk from me, and I had to change to bottle-feeding. It seemed that the stress from adjusting to a new environment and giving birth to our first child without the support of my own family had drained me physically and emotionally.

Our daughter had the croup frequently, which sounded horrible to me, the inexperienced mother. My mother-in-law taught me to put a slice of onion on a dish and place it over the pilot light of our gas stove, and after the onion juice began to appear, mix it with a spoonful of honey and give it to the baby for her cough. Her home remedy did work like magic.

My First Job

A few months after the birth of our first child, my mother-in-law thought I should do some work to bring in some income. Earle was going to school during the day and working at the railroad at night to supplement the meager GI Bill allotment and spending his little spare time he had golfing or going out with his old high school buddies. Earle and his brother, Hal, were the first generation of their family to go to college, thanks to the GI Bill. Since I had never worked in my life, and being bilingual in Japanese and English was not a marketable skill then, the only thing I knew was how to do was sew. In prewar Japan, sewing was a required course for all high school girls, and my mother had taught us three daughters to design and create our own wardrobes.

We bought a Singer sewing machine, black with shiny gold lettering, just as I remember my mother's prized possession from America. The difference was that all I had to do on my new electric machine was to gently step on a foot pedal, and it whirred along effortlessly. Although it was a lot of money for us then, it turned out to be the best investment we've made in our young life, as I made all of my and children's clothes and took in sewing as an extra income for years to come.

Earle's mother found a tailor in town, Mr. Glick, who was willing to give me a try. So, I left my infant daughter with my mother-in-law and took a bus into town, filled with fear and apprehension. Mr. Glick's tailor shop was small and dark, and three or four old women were bent over the sewing machines. Mr. Glick was a white-haired old man with thick glasses who spoke to me in a gentle voice. He gave me a pair of men's trousers and told me to shorten the length. He showed me how to hand stitch the hem. When I finished one, he looked it over, and said, "Make stitches smaller." He gave me another pair.

As I sat in a dark corner stitching men's trousers, I thought of my baby, and tears started to roll down my cheeks. *If my parents could see me now, what would they say!*

After a few hours, I could no longer contain myself and told Mr. Glick that I missed my daughter and wanted to go home. I don't think I even asked for any money. I just went home and never returned. When I look back, I think what a wimp I was, but adjusting to a new country, language, environment, customs, and values and being a new mother were enough experiences for me to handle at that time. I was simply not ready to go out to work.

I Want to Speak Japanese!

I missed my family. I missed speaking and hearing Japanese. I missed seeing my friends. I missed the familiar customs, sights, smells, and sounds of Japan. I missed Japanese food. Sushi was not yet in the American vocabulary.

It became a routine for me to put Julie down for a nap and just sit and watch the trees outside and sink into daydreaming. First, I would start with food—those delicious noodles, sushi, and Japanese bean cakes. Then my thoughts would turn to restaurants we used to frequent. Sometimes I could almost smell the freshly made sushi, oden, and special noodles. Then my mind would wander to our summer home in Oiwake, and there, my memories were endless. Every single memory in that "paradise" would return to my mind like a revolving lantern. I finally confided in my mother:

Dearest Mother,

I am going crazy with homesickness. Even if I sold all my possessions, it would not cover my plane ticket. Even for one week, I want to come home. I don't even feel like listening to my favorite music. Even when I have the time, I have no inclination to do anything. My mind is in chaos now. I don't want to worry Bunny, so I don't let on that I'm homesick. I haven't spoken Japanese for so long that sometimes my jaw is filled with tension and desire to speak Japanese until I cannot speak any more. You cannot imagine what it is like to have something to say, yet be unable to express your thoughts. I feel like Japanese words are all jammed up in my throat and mouth and cannot come out.

I miss the openness of the Japanese house, especially in the summer how the air flowed through the house when all the sliding doors are opened. Although American homes looked very open from outside as they have little or no fences like the Japanese homes, once inside, the Japanese homes are much more open as they have little walls. I miss the closeness to the outside where you just step out of the house and can be outside without having to go through narrow doors. I think the Japanese houses are more organic. I must admit, though, that I appreciate not having to use the mosquito net or contend with flies as all windows in American homes have screens ...

By the time Julie was six months old, I felt I could meet the challenge of becoming a seamstress. With my mother-in-law's help, I placed an ad in the paper. That week, I lived in fear and anxiety. Every time the phone rang, I would tense up, and my heart would start to pound for fear that I may not understand what the customer wanted. I didn't know the sewing terminology in English—not even the names of fabrics or styles.

Everyone seemed to speak extra quickly over the phone. After several failed attempts to get orders, I finally procured a couple. One was a summer dress for a hefty Russian lady who lived down the street, and the other was for making drapes. My mother-in-law encouraged me to take whatever came my way, as she would teach me how to do it. I even had to go to the customer's house to measure for the drapes. That was scary for me. Everyone seemed to be surprised when they met me. I think they were expecting a middle-aged woman, and instead, they got a young Japanese girl!

What I hated was to talk about the price. Americans did not hesitate to talk about money. In Japan, especially in samurai home, talking about money was considered dirty and vulgar. My in-laws thought I had quoted too low. So everyone got together and helped me decide how much I should charge for my work. They even called some seamstresses to get an idea. Finally, Earle's dad suggested that I should at least charge $1.00 an hour (This was 1950.). After making three dresses, I made $10.65! I promptly put it in our return-to-Japan fund. When we left Japan, seeing how distraught my mother and I were to face a separation that might be for life, Earle had told my mother, "Mama-san, I'll bring Nobuko back to Japan in five years when I finish school."

So, when we arrived in Champaign, we set up a bank account we called "return to Japan." Earle and I often talked of the day when we would go back to my home to live.

A Coat for $2.75!

A letter I wrote to my mother in early October 1950, two months before our son was born gives a glimpse of my life at 920 West Church Street, Champaign, Illinois:

Dear Mother,

I had a sleepless night and was thinking of home, and as if by magic, your letter arrived in the morning mail! So glad to hear that everyone is well. On October 8, Bunny took me to a concert by Rubinstein at the University. I wore my new dark green dress and wore alligator high heels Bunny's sister gave me. The program was mostly Chopin. What a treat!! I often play a Chopin album Bunny gave me for my birthday so I'm immersed in Chopin! I'm in heaven! … The other day Julie became ill, and I had to take her to a doctor. It was a very cold and rainy day, and she didn't own a coat but I only had $5. There is no such thing as a $5.00 coat! So I ran to a fabric store, bought some materials for $2.75, ran home, found for lining the leftover pink silk fabric from Berniece's blouse I made, and in 2 and a half hours, I put together a lined coat for Julie. Whew!! Of course, I had no time to hem it properly so I just basted it. Mother said, "Just roll it up when you take it off and nobody will notice it." American doctors are strict about being on time, so I was rushing there in the rain and slipped and fell and several people came to help me and the baby up. It's been a month, but my elbow still hurts. I have a tendency to rush around, and Bunny's family keeps telling me, "Faith, slow down! Don't get excited!" Living with Bunny's family has pluses and minuses. Just like we did in Tokyo, we tend to depend on them too much. We have to watch our budget, so I do not keep our refrigerator full. I try to buy only what we really need. But Bunny is like a child, and every time he can't find what he wants, he goes downstairs and raids his mother's fridge. I feel embarrassed and ashamed, so I have to spend extra for junk food

88

... so that Bunny won't keep running to his mom. I learned an American baby song called "Patty Cake" and taught it to Julie. It goes, "Patty Cake, patty cake, Baker's man, bake me a cake as fast as you can ..." She is so cute!! I love her so! Through my baby, I'm learning American culture!

I never told my American family or friends about my homesickness. I didn't want to appear ungrateful for their kindness or to worry them. This was the path I had chosen. For better or for worse, I had to face it and persevere. When someone asked me, "So, how do you like America?" I would give a cheerful answer with a big smile. Whenever I felt like crying, I would go to the bathroom, lock the door, and cry alone.

No Money but "Freedom"!

Although we were extremely frugal, the money was tight. My mother knew that we were financially struggling, and once in a while, she would procure American money from somewhere and slip a ten-dollar bill with her letter to me. In the summer of 1950, shortly before the arrival of our second child, I received a letter from my mother with money:

Dear Mother,

Thank you, thank you, and thank you for the $10.00 bill!! I had fun thinking what I could spend it on, and since I have only one pair of socks, decided to buy three pairs, and maybe a pair of shoes. But alas, after I bought the socks, the rest disappeared in buying food. I'm sorry, but believe me it was much needed and appreciated ...

We did manage to put away three hundred dollars from Earle's night job and bought a 1939 Dodge, but we had only a few dollars left to buy gasoline.

"Do you think we acted too hastily?" Earle wondered.

"Well, maybe, but it really does lift our spirit when we can go for a ride at the spur of the moment," I assured him.

We decided to sleep on it for a few days. It was a weekend, and it was a bright sunny day. We piled in the car and went for a drive. At night we went to a drive-in theater for a dollar without bothering my mother-in-law to babysit! I never dreamed that owning a car could give you such a sense of freedom and independence. I could finally understand why Americans were so car-crazy. We decided to keep the car and somehow manage to get enough money for the gas.

Birth of a Son

On October 26, 1950, twenty months after the birth of our daughter, our son was born. We named him Gary. This time I was psychologically better prepared. We had moved into Earle's brother's apartment after he and his wife with their infant son had moved to Ohio. It was only a two-room apartment, but it had many windows, a bigger kitchenette, and in general was much more cheery than the one we had previously been living in. I was up and about in no time and actually enjoying being a mother. I sent a telegram to my parents on the arrival of our new son.

With a toddler and an infant in a two-room apartment, my home sewing business became even more challenging. I did most of my work while the children were taking a nap or after they had gone to bed. Talking to customers on the phone was still a cause for anxiety. Face to face, I could understand most things, but on the phone everyone seemed to speak faster and to slur words together. Earle was still going to school, working nights, and spending weekends golfing or hanging out with his buddies. We began to see each other less and less.

With an additional member in the family, there was very little extra money to go around for entertainment. I learned a hundred ways to stretch a dollar. I made my own and my children's clothes. I got an old Navy pea jacket that Hal had worn during the war, took it apart, cleaned it, and made it over into my daughter's winter overcoat. In fact, Julie did not own a store-bought coat until she was in the third grade. The kids' toys were boxes, paper bags, clothespins, and pots and pans, which they learned to use with amazing creativity. At Christmas, Earle and I made toys for them. Earle's grandfather, father, and all of his uncles were carpenters. Having the "carpenter gene," Earle was quite handy with tools and could make a beautiful doll's cradle for our daughter or toys for our sons. Following the family tradition, before they were two, our sons Gary and Mark learned to use a real hammer. Both would later become fine cabinetmakers.

CHAPTER VIII: Making Soap out of Bacon Grease

Life moved slowly in a small college town in the 1950s and afforded me the chance to learn about everyday life in mid-America. Many aspects of life were similar to life in Japan—fathers went to work, mothers nurtured the family, and children went to school. One of the things that impressed me was how religious Americans were. Nearly everyone I met went to church on Sunday.

Also, just as peddlers in Japan used to come around selling tofu, roasted sweet potatoes, and even gold fish, calling out their trade or blowing a horn, in America, there were a Fuller Brush man, an egg man, a milkman on a horse-drawn wagon, and a Jewel coffee man. Early in the morning, you'd hear the clip-clop of horse's hooves on the street and the clanging sound of milk bottles (this was decades before plastic milk bottles). The egg man sometimes brought vegetables from his garden, and the Fuller Brush man had an array of brushes that I had never seen in my life. My mother-in-law was especially partial to the Jewel coffee.

The First Baptist Church

I was beginning to get the hang of running an "American" home, and decided to accompany Earle to his church with our children. Earle's father never went to church and slept in on Sundays. His mother went to a Methodist church with her youngest daughter. Earle went to a Baptist church, and he was a soloist in the choir. I joined the Women's Auxiliary and learned to take part in a bake sale and other church activities. Because Americans believed that "Japanese are so artistic," and I was, I was asked to be an assistant in the arts and crafts part of their summer Bible school. I learned about the three wise men and helped children make clay models of camels and palm trees with construction paper. Everyone admired them with exaggerated praise.

Children sometimes stared at me for a long time, as if trying to figure out who I was. There were no blacks, Hispanics, or Asians in the Baptist church we attended then. Most of the women have been going to the church together for a long time and knew each other intimately. The conversations frequently were about families and mutual friends whom I had never met. Although I did not feel completely at home, I made a point of not missing their ladies' meetings. The pastor used to visit us from time to time trying to convert me, the heathen from the Orient. I learned much about the American society through the church.

Learning How to Make Soap from Bacon Grease!

making soap from bacon grease and lye.

Having lived through the Great Depression, my mother-in-law was an extremely thrifty woman. My father-in-law had bacon and one egg every morning—this was decades before anyone talked about cholesterol—and Mother saved the bacon grease in a tall mason jar. When the jar got full, she made soap by adding lye to the bacon grease in a big washtub in the basement. I remember helping her stir the concoction with a long, wooden stick, feeling as if I were the witch brewing her magic potion. After several days, the brown goo would harden. We would loosen the formed chunk around the edges with a metal spatula and invert it onto a board. Then we'd cut it into many bars of brown soap, which we used both as hand soap and, grated, as laundry soap in the washing machine.

During the war years in Japan, when material shortage from food to clothing was so acute, we had learned to conserve, make do, or to go without. Having lived through this experience was a lifesaver for me, as after I came to America, I had to live with very limited funds; the lessons I'd learned also fitted nicely with my mother-in-law's thriftiness.

I helped my mother-in-law wash by hand lace curtains on their windows and learned to stretch them carefully on curtain stretchers, wooden contraptions with rows of tiny nails so that they would retain the original shape. When my sister-in-law was married, I made her wedding gown and the gowns for her bridesmaids as well. Since I did not learn any domestic skills at home, I followed my mother-in-law around like a puppy dog and learned how to run an American home. I think she was pleased that her new daughter-in-law, even though from another country, wanted to emulate her.

Although Mother and I shared similar life philosophies, we did have some differences of opinions in matters of women's education. I felt strongly that a woman should continue to study, even after motherhood. She felt that once a woman was married and had a family, that was enough. I wanted to take courses at the university, but she asked, "What for? Your family is everything."

It was not until decades later, when I became a grandparent, that I understood the true meaning of her words, "Your family is everything." I now know that not the grandest career, not fame nor fortune could take the place of a loving family. My mother-in-law was kind and thoughtful and wise. I owe a deep debt of gratitude to this wonderful woman.

Faith Nobuko Araki Barcus

Miss Kasuya, My Former College Professor

In the spring of 1951, Miss Kasuya, my former professor (later president) at Tsuda Juku College, wrote me that she was going on a seven-month tour of the colleges and universities in the United States, including her alma mater, Wellesley College in Massachusetts. When she visited the University of Illinois in Champaign, she came to see me at 920 West Church Street.

The last time we had seen each other was in Tokyo, more than six years earlier. I waited for her in front of our house on a cold, spring day. As she got out of the taxi, she gave me a cheerful, "Hello, Miss Araki!"

"Sensei!" I shouted and ran to her.

Meeting my husband and the children, Miss Kasuya seemed genuinely happy for me; she seemed pleased to see that I was surviving all right in my new country. After she returned to Japan, she published a newspaper article about our meeting, noting her observations on Japanese women who married American soldiers and immigrated to the United States and her visit. She wrote: "When I stopped at the University of Illinois to visit their library, I had an opportunity to see my former student, Miss Nobuko Araki, now, Mrs. E. Barcus, who lives in Champaign, Illinois. She had immigrated to America in 1948, and is now the mother of two lovely children. She told me how disappointed she was at first as life in America was nothing like what she had imagined. I could sense the struggles she had gone through adjusting to the new environment, living with her in-laws, and caring for her two young children. But she has faith in her husband and is determined to succeed. Ms. Araki said they had saved enough money to buy their first car. If every Japanese woman who enters into international marriage has the kind of conviction and determination as Miss Araki has, they will succeed. (September 3, 1950. Sunday edition. Newspaper name unclear.)

Ms. Kasuya's article about meeting me in Illinois.

After Ms. Kasuya returned to Japan, my mother went to see her and was relieved to hear from someone who had actually seen me and could describe my life in America.

Different Values

As I became familiar with American culture and customs, I realized that traditional American and Japanese beliefs about humanity's relationship to nature differed. Americans believed that humankind was the master of the earth, and nature was something that needed to be conquered at humankind's Will. This is just the opposite of the Buddhist teaching that humanity is a part of nature and needs to coexist peacefully with all other living things on this earth, similar to the American Indian's beliefs.

I suppose a nation's values and philosophy are forged, to a large extent, by its geography and history. It became clear to me that a nation that was begun by a people of the hunter stock, seeking religious freedom and fighting persecution, would have a strong religious belief and a fighting spirit. Their Christian belief in humankind's dominance over nature bred the unique "pioneer spirit" and tamed this colossal and rich land. It was also evident that having such enormous "elbow room" created the big and generous-hearted people I encountered in my new home. Over the years, as a multitude of races and ethnic groups joined the pursuit of happiness, of building a Utopian nation with democracy as their common goal, it is understandable that such a diverse group, who call themselves Americans, also cherish their own private spaces by being assertive and defending their rights.

On the other hand, Japan is a tiny island with little natural resources, inhabited by a people of agrarian stock who slowly evolved over more than two millennia, sharing and "making do" with what little they had. It makes sense that these people would develop a cooperative spirit and strong group cohesion. It is not easy to celebrate what one does not have, but the Japanese have elevated what they don't have to a high art form, celebrating simplicity and smallness. The Buddhist enlightenment of "Nothingness is everything" (Satori) fitted in nicely with Japan's lack of natural resources. The Japanese belief in sharing nature with other living things helped to develop the people's unique love of nature and a kinship with all life on earth. My mother used to teach me to honor and love flowers, trees, and the smallest of insects.

If we likened America to a luxury ocean liner with an enormous space and luxurious trappings, Japan might be likened to a small, wooden rowboat with people crammed in. The ocean liner would confidently glide across the vast ocean, each occupant having ample space to develop his or her own individuality using his or her rich resources. On the other hand, the occupants of the wooden boat would have to row in unison, without pause, to keep it afloat, sharing what they have, and not allowing any occupant to stand up demanding his or her rights, for it might capsize their boat.

These almost opposite views on nature were clearly demonstrated to me one spring afternoon. Feeling released from the winter's grip, my in-laws and I were out in the backyard. We saw a group of ants busily carrying their provisions to and from their home near the garage. To me, this was a sign of spring, a time to rejoice. "Oh, look, ants are out!" I said and bent down to watch them.

To my horror, everyone's shoes came down on them and squished them. To my American family, ants were a nuisance that did damage to human dwellings. I recalled an essay I wrote when I was in grade school about how I'd rescued a cricket that fell into our swimming pool by throwing a big leaf for it to climb on. I thought of elaborate funerals and burials we'd performed for our dead goldfish when we were children and how shocked I'd been to learn that Americans flushed dead goldfish down the toilet. As I slowly learned what makes America tick, I was determined to take the best of both cultures to make my own unique culture. But it would take decades of trials and errors.

CHAPTER IX: A TRIP OF A LIFETIME

Reunion

The spring of 1952, four years after I arrived in the United States, held my darkest hours. My inexplicable allergy was still acting up, and my homesickness was so great. That is when I received news that my parents were planning a trip around the world for business and pleasure. The impetus for the trip was the American Management Association Convention in New York City, which my father was to attend. My parents decided to go to Europe as well. The seven-year occupation by the Allied forces had ended, and the Japanese had resumed self-government and were able to travel outside of Japan. My father, accompanied by my mother and his business associate, headed out to see the world, and they planned to stop in Champaign on their way! It had been four years since I had seen my parents, and my heart was filled with gladness.

They left Yokohama on *M.S. Hikawa-maru* on April 24, arriving in Los Angeles on May 8. They were to cross America by air and train and depart for Europe from New York by ship. The trip was combination business and sentimental journey for my father. On the business side, he wanted to see what was happening in the postwar United States in terms of technology and how it affected the lives of its citizens.

He also wanted to retrace his footsteps to the time of his youth when he'd studied in 1918 America. He planned business trips to Chicago to meet with railway executives, to Detroit to study the automobile industry, to Cornell University to see their hotel management program, to the Tennessee Valley Authority to witness its technological triumph, and to the headquarters of Remington Rand to learn about their cutting-edge technology in communication.

On the personal side, he planned to see me; visit his alma mater, Akron University in Ohio; and stop in to see the efficiency expert, Mrs. Lillian Gilbreth, in New Jersey before arriving in New York for the AMA convention. He planned to travel through Europe to see how the rest of the world had recovered from the World War II.

My father was astounded by the technological progress the United States had made since his student days in 1918 to 1920. He was in awe of the Golden Gate Bridge, which had been built with new technology. He wrote of this particular experience in his book, *History of Efficiency Management*:

> The toll is 25 cents per car, and the daily take is said to be about $5000.00. It cost $18,000,000 to build, so they have already recovered the cost. America is a country that never forgets to make a profit no matter what they undertake ...[6]

He was also amazed at the rapid development of highways in the United States. Characteristically, he figured out all the statistics of railway travel versus automobile travel, and why people preferred automobile travel and why the railroads were running in the red. He predicted that, within fifty years, passenger trains might become obsolete in America.

The great leap in communication systems in America astounded him also. He noted in his book that, in America, one need not shout on the long-distance telephone calls. The trouble-free international calls, he reported, were due to the dust-free and climate-controlled environment of the operators' rooms and the small size of the cables, which enabled the phone companies to service more lines economically. Were he alive today, I wonder what he would say of the electronic communication age.

Hollywood

The diary my mother kept chronicles this journey around the world. She wrote of that, in Los Angeles, a limousine delivered my parents and my father's business associate to the Twentieth Century Fox studio to

---

[6]   *History of Efficiency Management, 1971.* Page 133

meet with a Mr. Bishop, the director of the International Department. My mother presented a Japanese doll to Ms. Linda Darnell, a popular star at the time. She also met Patricia Neal, another 1950s star, who was shooting some scenes in an upcoming movie. My parents were amazed at the scale and detail of the various studio sets, from "saloons" in cowboy movies to "mountains" and "forests" in adventure movies. Being a "dress designer," mother took meticulous notes on how Hollywood women— from the stars to lowly office girls—dressed. While my father was busy with business meetings, my mother went on a guided shopping tour in Beverly Hills. She liked seeing the newest fashions in America, but shopping, unfortunately, was not the kind of activity she enjoyed. She probably would have preferred visiting an art museum or going hiking.

Tearful Reunion

On May 19, Earle and I drove with our three-year old daughter to Chicago to meet my parents at the Chicago Hilton, leaving our two-year old son with my mother-in-law in Champaign. (My third child, a son, was not yet born.) Earle and I waited in the lobby with Julie, in her Sunday best—a pale blue organdy dress trimmed in lace that I'd designed and made and shiny black patent leather shoes. Our eyes were set on the elevators.

Then I saw them, my mother in a white summer suit with blue polka dots and a white hat and my father in a white linen summer suit and white shoes. I jumped to my feet and shouted, "Okaasama! Otohsama! [Mother! Father!]"

"Oh, Nobuko-chan!" my mother cried out, her eyes filling with tears of joy.

This was the first time my parents had seen their granddaughter. "So, this is our little Julie!" my mother exclaimed. "What a beautiful little girl!"

Even though I had shown my daughter photos of her grandparents many times, actually meeting them in person, in an unfamiliar environment, was a bit scary for three-year-old Julie. She clung to my skirt and peeked out from behind me.

"Bunny-san!" my mother said, turning to my husband. "How are you?"

"Hello, Mama-san, Mr. Araki!" Earle called in turn.

My parents warmly shook hands with Earle.

It was an emotional reunion with tears flowing freely but with few words. We were simply overcome with the joy of seeing each other after four years.

My parents were surprised to see me thin and pale, but I told them it was from fatigue, as we had been painting our apartment to welcome them to Champaign. My mother and I talked well into the night, catching up on all the news back home. She talked about my friends, who continued to visit my mother to give encouragement and support in my absence. Mother thought I needed a vacation and suggested that they could curtail their European trip and take the children and me back to Japan with them for some R & R.

I felt that, if I went back to Japan with them, I may not return to America and declined her offer without giving her the real reason. I also knew that my children of mixed races would fare much better in America than in Japan, where even slightly different people were often ostracized.

At Chicago Hilton with my parents, Earle's sister, husband and friend.

A New Plan

After seeing my life in Champaign with their own eyes and meeting my in-laws and American friends, my parents, I think, were relieved that I lived among good people. I did not have a lot of time with my father, who was busy visiting various companies and factories and also being a guest speaker at the local Rotary Club wherever they stopped. But, many months later, I learned in a letter from my friend that he was a keen observer.

My friend wrote, "Your father told me with tears in his eyes that he saw you using a comb with missing teeth and remarked how modest your circumstances must be …"

My mother was shocked to see my empty closet, as she remembered me as a real clotheshorse in my youth.

My parents wanted to see more of America and also to visit my father's alma mater and old friends in Akron, Ohio. They proposed a plan. If Earle would drive and act as my father's secretary, they would pay all the expenses for Earle and me to travel to and from New York. Earle had just finished his bachelor's degree in economics, and was willing to miss his graduation ceremony for this unexpected offer. He talked it over with his parents, and they agreed to care for our two children for a month.

The Invisible Hand of Destiny

On June 7, we arrived in Akron. My father wanted to see the chemistry lab where he'd spent many hours in his youth; visit the Hoffman's where he'd lodged; and see the Naugles, who'd run a neighborhood diner where he had most of his meals and who had treated him as if he were their own son more than thirty years earlier. The houses were still there, but the Hoffmans had moved on, and the Naugles had retired to Pennsylvania. To his delight, the chemistry lab was exactly the same as he remembered it.

As we were strolling through the campus, a tall American with a big smile approached us and said, "Hello. You must be Mr. Araki!"

We were speechless. The man, it turned out, had received my father's letter to the chemistry department advising of his visit to Akron sometime in June.

More surprisingly, the day turned out to be alumni day! We were invited to attend a function that night in the school's auditorium. Surprise of all surprises, there were Professor Simmons, my father's mentor of thirty years earlier, and Professor Schmidt of the chemistry department, now white-haired and retired.

After the entertainment, suddenly all the lights came on and lit the auditorium as if in bright daylight. Professor Simmons stood on the stage, and said, "Dear Akron alumni! I have an extraordinary announcement to make. In 1920, I had a graduate student named Araki from Japan who came to study rubber chemistry under my tutelage. So much has happened in our lives since then, and we lost touch with each other. I remember Araki as not only a brilliant student but a man of uncommon character. Today, I'm honored to introduce to you my former protégé, Araki, and his family, who are traveling through the United States. Here they are, Mr. and Mrs. Araki, their daughter Nobuko, and her American husband, Mr. Barcus. Please give them a warm welcome!"

We all stood up and bowed, amidst a thunderous applause.

Professor Simmons continued, "I might add that Araki wins the award for the alum who traveled the farthest!"

More applause followed. Many people came to extend their warm welcome to us, showering my father with questions.

We met Mrs. Simmons, wife of Professor Simmons, a friendly white-haired lady who remembered my father as a man who marched to his own drum. "Yes, your father was a character! I remember him floating in the river on an inner tube reading a book and holding an umbrella to shield the sun!"

My father laughed, "I did that? I do not remember!"

Mother, Earle, and I left the professors and my father to reminisce about the good old days and returned to our hotel. My father returned quite late, his eyes shining with the excitement of meeting his dear old professors and reliving his youth. He told me that this was the happiest day of his life.

My father's reunions with his past continued. We were able to locate Mr. and Mrs. Naugle's Pennsylvania address, and my father called them. Of course they would be most happy to see their "Frank," as my father was known to them. So we took a winding road off of a main highway to a small village in Pennsylvania. The Naugles lived in a tiny, modest home. The white-haired, friendly couple welcomed us warmly.

Mrs. Naugle had baked a lemon pie for the occasion, and we witnessed another joyous and tearful reunion—this one between my father and his long-lost American "family." The sweet elderly couple remembered, with affection, the generous and kind young Japanese man who had frequented their diner so many years ago.

After that, Mrs. Naugle and I corresponded regularly for several years until her death. She told me, in the neat penmanship the people in olden days had learned in school, filling the letter paper from corner to corner, of her vegetable gardens, her grandchildren, and Mr. Naugle's arthritis. She always signed her letter, "Ma Naugle." I told her about my growing children, my life in America, and my father in Tokyo.

Mrs. Lillian Gilbreth

**Top: Mother and Father with Mrs. Gilbreath at her home in New Jersey.
Below, Mrs. Gilbreath and father behind, 1929 Scientific Mgmt Conference**

前列左から
ギルブレス夫人
河 田 重 氏
後列左から
荒 木 東 一 郎
根 上 耕 一

東京で開催の万国工業会議
第12部会（Scientific mana-
gement）へ出席のギルブレ
ス夫人のために
　　昭4. 11. 20. 日本鋼管にて

108

It was as if we were reliving my father's student days. The amazing reunions did not end in Pennsylvania. In Boston, we stayed at Hotel Bostonian and made the rounds of the sites my father had once visited.. My father reminisced about those carefree days as we visited the "Boston Tech," as the MIT was called in earlier days. He introduced us to the Boston Pops at the Symphony Hall and the magnificent pipe organs and the Mapparium at the Christian Science Mother Church.

I stayed at the hotel to catch up on laundry and some shopping, and Earle drove my parents to New Jersey to see Mrs. Lillian Gilbreth, wife of Frank Gilbreth, the pioneer in time and motion efficiency method. Lillian Gilbreth had been my father's mentor back in 1920 when he studied at the Gilbreth's laboratory at the Massachusetts Institute of Technology. She had continued her husband's work after his death. The last time my father had seen Mrs. Gilbreth was in 1929 in Tokyo, Japan, when she'd attended the International Scientific Management Conference.

My mother wrote in her diary of her meeting Mrs. Gilbreth:

June 21, Saturday, Cloudy

We left Nobuko to do some shopping, and Bunny drove us to New Jersey to visit Mrs. Lillian Gilbreth. We went through the Lincoln Tunnel, which connects New Jersey and New York. It is the largest and longest underground tunnel for passenger automobiles only. Mrs. Gilbreth, now close to eighty, has a little difficulty walking, but her mind is sharp. Her motherly demeanor put me at ease immediately. She shook my hand with such warmth and friendship that I could not help feeling drawn to her as if I had known her all my life. She served a cake she baked herself, and the conversation flourished, reminiscing about the past and critiquing the present. She lives alone in an apartment with a bedroom, living room, dining room, study, and music room. I was particularly impressed with her study, whose walls were filled with books overflowing into the hallway. She said she is catching a plane in the afternoon for her lecture tour. She laughed that she probably sleeps on the plane more than she does in her bed at home. We took pictures in her music room. Chopin was open on the piano, which gladdened my heart and made me feel even closer to Mrs. Gilbreth, Chopin being

109

my favorite composer. On the piano were the pictures of her twelve children, each looking healthy and prosperous. I was not only awed by this remarkable woman who was still living a life of purpose but felt a little envious.

At the Stock Exchange

We stopped at Cleveland, Syracuse, Niagara Falls, Cornell University in Ithaca, and Boston, some places for sightseeing and others on my father's business. In New York City, we went to the New York Stock Exchange. In a rather rushed atmosphere, lots of people came, introduced themselves, and disappeared quickly before we had a chance to understand who was who. I guess the people who work in the stock exchange have to be quick and on the go at all times. We were tired from a long trip, and although we felt honored to be given a private tour of the Stock Exchange and the showing of their public relations film in their small theater, after a small talk in a plush office, we were glad to thank and leave these good but busy people. After we got on the elevator, my father asked the attendant who was assigned to us. "Who was that man I was talking to in his office?"

"Oh," the attendant responded, "he is the president of the Stock Exchange!"

The American Management Association Convention was held at the Waldorf Astoria Hotel. My father had registered Earle as part of his party, and together, they attended the luncheon. Earle was just a "kid" out of college and felt completely out of place sitting among powerful CEOs and entrepreneurs. He did not even own a dress shirt and made do with a short sleeve, white shirt. I think he was a bit self-conscious about his arms sticking out of his cheap Sears summer suit without the shirtsleeves and cuff links.

To Earle's dismay, as he is a proud man, my father tried his best to drum up a job opportunity for Earle wherever he went, as any good Japanese father-in-law would do. He could not understand why Earle wouldn't appreciate his efforts. When we were in Chicago, he wanted to take Earle along to a meeting with some big shots in railways so that he could introduce his son-in-law for possible employment.

"I appreciate your concern for my future employment, Mr. Araki, but I would like to explore that at a later date on my own," Earle said.

My father, annoyed that his greenhorn son-in-law didn't understand the value of a good connection, which was everything in getting good jobs in Japan, insisted that Earle accompany him.

He refused and they almost came to a blow.

After a hectic, month-long journey with my parents, Earle and I said good-bye to them in Washington DC and drove back to Champaign. The trip back with just the two of us—no busy daily agendas or children—gave us much-needed time to replenish our relationship.

CHAPTER X: CIRCLE OF LIFE

Home Sweet Home

In the spring of 1953, I was eligible for my American citizenship. I had been studying the history and political structure of the United States, and, as a sign of my commitment to our marriage, I decided to apply. I took the test, passed, and was sworn in. I was now an American citizen. I made "Faith," the English translation of my Japanese name Nobuko, my legal name. It *was* my faith in myself and in people around me that had helped me through many challenges in my American journey.

The same year, we moved out of Earle's family home on Church Street and into the graduate students' housing of the University of Illinois. Stadium Terrace had served as army barracks built for soldiers during the war. When the swarm of returning GIs had entered the university on the GI Bill, the barracks were converted into student housing for a rent of sixty dollars a month. Each unit had three living quarters, each outfitted with a tin box of a shower and a big, gas space heater in the middle of the living room. There was no central heating. Each unit was given a letter of the alphabet: A, B, and C. We were in 49-B, the middle unit at number 49. There was a patch of dirt in front of each unit with a flimsy wire fence around it. This was our "yard."

The barracks had been put together hastily. The walls were thin, the windows rattled in winter, and the cold Illinois winter wind blew in through the chinks. But it was our first home sweet home. Although my in-laws were good people, it was good to be alone with Earle after five years, and the move gave me a sense of freedom and a true feeling of a "family." It seemed to signify a new beginning for me.

Going Home Some Day

The promise to return to Japan in five years after Earle finished school had, in retrospect, been an improbable dream, voiced only to soothe everyone, but it became a kind of a game to think of ways to make a living utilizing our Japan-America ties. In the end, new plans came into our life. When Earle finished school, he decided to go on to graduate school. When he got his master's degree, his professor urged him to go for his PhD. Our return-to-Japan plan was postponed again.

My Saddest Day

Early in the morning of August 11, 1954, as the rays of the bright summer sun pierced between the cracks of our cheap window shades and we were beginning to wake up, the telephone rang. I ran to it rubbing sleep out of my eyes, with a sense of foreboding at such an early call. It was my elder sister, Keiko.

"Nobuko-chan, I have a bad news for you ..." she began haltingly. "Mother passed away last night ..."

I put my hand over my mouth to stifle a cry.

"Are you there?"

"Yes. How did she die?"

"Well, we are not sure until the autopsy. Probably complications from the stomach surgery she had earlier in the year. She has not been feeling well, and it's been so hot ... couldn't eat ..."

Holding back the tears, I asked, "Did she suffer?"

"I don't think so. I was out running some errands, and Mother was at home alone in bed. When I came home, she was unconscious. We rushed her to the hospital. The doctors tried everything they could, but she never regained consciousness."

I bit my lips and swallowed a cry and said in a trembling voice, "Okay, I understand. Thanks, Keiko."

In a tearful, almost inaudible voice, my sister added, "Father says we will have a small family service ... and since you have two kids ... and no money and ... it would take too long for him to arrange for money for your airfare to be sent to you, ... if you can't return, he'll understand."

I sat in the kitchen and cried softly, not wanting to wake anyone. Images of the past, memories of my mother rushed in, swirling around in my head—her special delicate scent when she wore kimono; going to the art museum, concerts, or hiking; our dance parties and haiku parties; how she would happily pour over a fashion book from America and design our dresses. She was a naturalist, artist, designer, and poet—a romantic. She showed us the beauty of nature and taught us to honor it. She taught us to cherish good books and always have a dream.

I finally gathered myself and put the kettle on to make myself a cup of tea. Earle came out, rubbing his sleepy eyes. "What are you doing so early in the morning?" he asked.

"My mother died. Keiko just called me." I started to cry.

"Oh no! I'm so sorry." Earle hugged me tightly and kissed me. I stayed in his embrace for a long time, drawing comfort from it, until the bubbling sound of water boiling brought me back to reality.

Circle of Life

A year after my mother's death, as if her spirit was trying to lift me out of my sorrow, I became pregnant. And in 1956, I gave birth to our third child, a son, Mark. It had been six years since Gary was born. This time, I was more experienced in mothering; my life was more stable, and consequently, Mark was a happy child, and he did lift me from my depression. To Julie, then eight years old, Mark was like having a live doll to play with. Six-year-old Gary felt a big brotherly responsibility. He showed Mark the ropes of being a boy.

Earle, after earning his master's degree at the University of Illinois, at the recommendation of his professor, decided to go for his PhD and got a teaching assistant position. The GI Bill had run out long before, and he took out a school loan. We had again put aside our promise of returning to Japan when Earle "finished school." In retrospect, in spite of tight money, I think the Stadium Terrace years were fairly peaceful.

One-Room School House

At the end of a dirt road that ran at the edge of our "village" was a one-storied, simple wooden structure. I'm not sure what it was used for before. It was rather barren, with windows all around and the bathrooms in the basement. Perhaps it was once a classroom for the soldiers. When we were there, it was the classroom for the first graders from Stadium Terrace and nearby farms. Mrs. Knapp, a crisp, no-nonsense, middle-aged woman with a divine sense of humor was the teacher, nurse, and janitor in this one-room schoolhouse called, for some unknown reason, "Percival."

Our daughter, on her first day of school, proudly told Mrs. Knapp, "I know how to spell 'beautiful,' and I finished reading *Black Beauty*." Julie was a precocious child who started reading cereal boxes at the breakfast table before she was barely able to walk, had exceptionally developed verbal skills, and never stopped talking. After a while, she became Mrs. Knapp's able assistant, and whenever Mrs. Knapp had to leave the room, she would leave the children in Julie's care.

There was one thing that scared my daughter at the school—the bathroom. It was in the dark basement and gave her a spooky feeling. Julie would hold her nature's call as long as she could and run home during a lunch break.

Mrs. Knapp's husband was a professor at the university, and her children were grown and gone. She combined book learning with life learning, taking the children to visit neighborhood farms or to meadows nearby. The building was stark and the school supplies modest, but I think this first year at Percival was the best education our daughter and son received.

One day, Mrs. Knapp asked us if we would allow Julie to be put in the longitudinal "gifted children" project at the university. Researchers planned to follow, for decades, a group of children with exceptional gifts to see what kind of adults they'd become. The project was discontinued many years later due to lack of funds. After Percival, Julie skipped the second grade and was placed in the third grade in a public school in town. It was not until after she finished the third grade that we found out that she had missed learning cursive writing, which was taught in the second grade. She never told anyone, and just went along with the rest of the class as if she knew what she was doing. She must have inherited my *gambaru* (persevering) spirit!

Beer and Bridge

The resident students in Stadium Terrace were nearly all returning veterans who were starting their families. We were all in the same boat—we had no money, but we had great hope. The row after row of barracks swarmed with little children. While the men studied, the wives tended the home hearth, found a million ways to stretch a dollar, shared parenting knowledge and support, forged friendships, and dreamed of a better life to come.

We bought a used wringer-type washing machine and put it in our kitchenette, which was an extension of the living room. We dried our clothes on the lines in the backyard, and in winter, we either hung them outside where they'd freeze or inside, like layers and layers of banners in the living room. Sometimes when we were not careful, we got our heads caught in the low lines. For entertainment, we visited each other's homes, played bridge, drank beer, and if we didn't have enough money for beer, we had tea. Exchanging babysitting was easy, and sometimes Earle and I went to the university's free Friday night mixers and danced the night away to the DJ music. Because the residents at Stadium Terrace shared a common dream, I think people were exceptionally charitable and supportive of one another.

My American Friends

Through friendships I made with many women in Stadium Terrace, slowly I learned what it is to be an American. These women were bright, intelligent, caring, and diverse. My next-door neighbor, Eileen, a former school teacher, was a big, plain-speaking, down-to-earth woman, a typical midwesterner. Her husband, Jim, who served in the army during World War II, was also a slow-speaking, earthy midwesterner. Jim was working on his bachelor's degree on the GI Bill, and the couple was raising three daughters. Our daughter and son forged a close friendship with the girls, and the kids went to the same one-room school nearby.

Eileen was like a big tree that I could lean on for support and shade for me from the sun. She made me feel safe and comfortable. The Japanese *amae* raised its ugly head, and I began to depend on her too much without realizing it. We both belonged to the university wives bridge club, and I began to take it for granted that she'd always drive us to the bridge session.

One day, she said as we were taking down the laundry in the backyard, "Oh, Faith, I won't be going to the bridge game this week. So, you'll have to find your ride."

I was shaken. "Oh, what should I do? I don't know anybody else going from here," I said.

"Maybe Earle could take you over and you can find a ride back. I'm sure someone will be going from Stadium Terrace, maybe not in our block. Faith," she added. "I don't want you to assume that I'm going to provide your transportation every time."

This is how Eileen taught me, by telling me directly what was acceptable and what was not. She would gently nudge me away from her whenever I became too dependent on her.

A skinny, blonde woman named Fay lived across the street. "Just being a wife doesn't mean you are automatically a good cook," she would declare, as she chain-smoked. "I hate cooking! I told Tom when I got married not to expect any good home cooking, she'd add with a laugh.

I asked Fay, "What did Tom say?"

"Oh, he said that was okay and that he would do the cooking," Fay would reply, laughing.

Such openness for a woman was shocking but at the same time refreshing to me. I made mental notes of every word, every gesture of these diverse American women.

Gentle Wendy in the end unit with a scientist husband wrapped me with her kindness and a sweet smile. I met Catholics, Protestants, Jews, and nonbelievers.

Some women were as gentle and wispy as a spring breeze, and some were strong and fearless. But not all were kind to me. There was a childless woman, a friend of Eileen's, who lived in the barracks three rows over. Whenever she came to visit Eileen and I happened to be in our "yard," I would smile and say "hello." But she never responded. She just looked at me with her cold eyes and disappeared into Eileen's barracks.

Some months later, I finally got up enough courage and asked, "Eileen, that friend who comes to your house doesn't like me. She never says hello when I try to speak to her. Did I do something to offend her?"

Eileen told me that her friend's brother was killed in the Pacific, and she still had a lot of anger and hatred toward any Japanese.

It was the friendship with Bertha and Mary that cracked open the door to independence for me. Bertha was a crackerjack legal secretary who went on working part-time after her son was born. She was bright, articulate, organized, efficient, and thoughtful, and fearless. She simply exuded confidence. I think I was a little in awe of her. Mary had polio when she was a child and walked with crutches. Her legs had atrophied, but her shoulders were strong from maneuvering herself with crutches for so many years. She was immaculately well groomed at all times. Her beautifully manicured red nails impressed me. She was also bright, articulate, organized, efficient, and thoughtful, and she never allowed her disability to hamper her life. She was an inspiration to me. Both women had sons the same age as my last child, Mark.

We decided to take turns babysitting and attend some classes at the university. I had been hungry for intellectual challenge and welcomed this opportunity. This was the first time I had attended an American university, and also a coed school. I was a bit fearful and intimidated. Although I had been in America for nearly ten years and had plunged myself into joining a church women's organization, a university women's club, and even becoming a den mother for my son's Cub Scouts, speaking up in a coed class was a mountain I still could not climb. A psychology professor wrote "B+" on my grade postcard and scribbled below, "If you had participated in class, you'd have gotten an A." My silence in class had cost me a grade.

CHAPTER XI:
BOSTON, HERE WE COME!

Good-bye, Champaign, Hello Boston

In 1959, eleven years after I came to America, Earle completed his PhD program in communications at the University of Illinois and began the search for a real job. There was an offer in Hawaii that looked good. I don't remember why we did not pursue this. Perhaps we felt Hawaii was not quite real Ameica ...? In any case, we went to Missouri for an interview in Jefferson City. The job looked great, but I was reluctant to settle in such a rural setting. Having grown up in a big city, I had not been completely happy living in Champaign, and spending the rest of my life in another small town was an option I wanted to avoid.

Then came an offer from Boston University. The image of Boston that prevailed among midwesterners portrayed the city as old, formal, conservative, snobbish, and elite,—almost a foreign country that was not quite American. We were more than a little afraid of how a racially mixed family would be accepted in such a "proper" city. But my desire to live in a big city again was stronger than our concerns about the unknown reception in Boston, and I strongly urged Earle to take the position.

In August 1959, we sold or gave away our meager furniture and belongings, piled our three kids into our 1949 Chevrolet with our earthly possessions tied on top of the car, and left Champaign for good. We did not even have a home in Boston, but with our youthful optimism—we were only in our thirties—we figured something would turn up.

The Hub of the Universe

With three children, the youngest not yet four, there was always laundry to be done, and the going was slow. We took our time getting to our new home, stopping and seeing some sights along the way as a kind of vacation, a luxury we hadn't had in a long time. A week later, we arrived in Boston at night. As we drove around looking for a hotel, a neon sign reading, Hotel Bostonian, jumped into our vision.

"Hey! Isn't that the hotel we stayed in when we traveled with our parents in 1952?" I asked Earle.

"Yeah, right. Your father said it was a first-rate hotel in his student days, and I remember it was comfortable when we stayed there seven years ago," he said enthusiastically as he was exhausted from the long drive and was anxious to end the search.

We walked in and saw the lobby dimly lit and looking shabbier than when we'd stayed with my parents in 1952. Seamy-looking men loitered and watched us with hard, suspicious eyes.

Earle whispered, "It doesn't look as nice as it did before. What do you think?"

"Well," I replied, "the kids are so tired, and I'm sure you are too. It will only be a few days. Let's stay!"

Our children clung to us, and we stayed close together. We got on the elevator, which had seen better days. We asked for a double occupancy room and a rollaway bed for our daughter, and we decided that the boys would share one double bed, and Earle and I the other. The room was large, neat, and clean, but the drapes and bedding showed signs of wear. Nevertheless, we were so tired that we all just crawled into the beds and fell fast asleep.

Many days later, we found out that Hotel Bostonian had fallen on hard times and had become a hotel for prostitutes who brought their "clients"! We stayed there for three days catching up on laundry until the university housing people found an apartment for us in a suburb called Brookline. Later that year, we discovered an amazing coincidence— in the summer of 1921, my father had lodged with a family named Wheeler in Brookline while he studied at Frank Gilbreth's time and motion efficiency laboratory at Massachusetts Institute of Technology. The invisible hand of destiny seemed to be at work again.

To my delight, I found Boston to be a hospitable city, with all the cultural amenities of a large city without the hassle. There were world-class museums, a concert hall, libraries, hospitals, universities, and numerous historical sites. The quaint trolley cars that crisscrossed the city reminded me of the trolley cars in prewar Tokyo, and the charming red brick old-England architecture captured my heart. I felt I had found a city of my heart's desire.

The old five-bedroom apartment on the second and third floors of a duplex near Coolidge Corner in Brookline seemed like a palace to us, who were used to the three-room barracks with a tin-box shower and a space heater. We had central heating, an old but spacious bathroom with a claw-footed bathtub, and a clothesline with a pulley that went out of our kitchen window to a big tree in the back just like I had seen in some foreign movies. The apartment was sparsely but adequately furnished with a hard sofa and old bureaus, but to us it seemed quite luxurious, as we did not own a stick of furniture. The neighborhood was filled with tall shade trees and was built on a hill called Corey Hill, where we had a panoramic view of Boston. It was a safe neighborhood with lots of children.

Earle started his first *real* job at Boston University; Julie and Gary were enrolled in Devotion School, a fine public school nearby; and I set out to learn the lay of the land with my three-year-old Mark in tow.

Coolidge Corner reminded me of the neighborhood in Tokyo, with many small mom-and-pop stores where I got to know the owners.

Mrs. Levy, our stout landlady, lived downstairs with two boarders: Mr. Webber, a tall elderly, gentleman, and Rachel, a young Jewish woman with troubled eyes and tattooed numbers on her arm who had been a survivor of the Holocaust. Just as my father had been lucky in finding such goodhearted American families who took him in as a part of the family when he was a student in 1920, I was lucky in finding these kind and goodhearted people as our housemates in 1959. Mrs. Levy taught me where to shop, how to cook potato pancakes, and about our neighbors, who included an eccentric old violinist in the Boston Symphony Orchestra who called me, "Mon Cherie!" whenever we met on the street.

God Bless the Children's Hospital!

One day, shortly after we had moved in, I was scrubbing down the bathroom. Mark came running in, tripped on the bottle of Clorox (glass in those days), and gashed his foot. The blood splattered all over the floor. I picked him up and made sure no glass was in his foot, wrapped his foot with towels, and ran downstairs and banged on Mrs. Levy's door.

"Mrs. Levy! Mrs. Levy, I need help!"

Mr. Webber answered the door. "What is the matter, Faith?" he asked.

I quickly explained the situation and showed our son with the blood-soaked towel wrapped around his foot.

"Oh my God," said Mr. Webber." "Come in, come in! I'll call the police!"

I heard Mr. Webber calling 9-1-1. Within minutes, I heard the siren, and two officers from the Brookline police arrived. They put Mark and me in their cruiser and sped through the streets of Boston with a siren wailing and the blue lights flashing. The speed and efficiency with which the doctors and nurses responded at the hospital took my breath away. The doctor who expertly stitched up the gash said Mark couldn't have tripped on a better bottle, as Clorox disinfected the cut immediately. This was my introduction to the world famous Boston Children's Hospital.

This was not the only time I would be indebted to Brookline Police Department and the Children's Hospital. The following year, ten-year-old Gary decided to go through the apartment without touching the floor. I could never fathom how boys and men could come up with ideas that were so outrageous and foolhardy. He hopped from chair to couch to chair to banister, and as he was swinging from a doorway to the living room, his hands slipped, and he fell into the French door, shattering the glass. His foot had gone through the glass pane.

Again, I ran downstairs and knocked on Mrs. Levy's door. "Mrs. Levy," I called. "Mrs. Levy, I need help!"

Again, Mrs. Levy was out, and Mr. Webber answered the door. "Mr. Webber, Gary is hurt! He put his leg through the glass door!"

"What," Mr. Webber exclaimed. "How did he do that?"

I felt a little embarrassed, but I explained, "He was jumping from the couch to the doorway."

"Oh my gosh; I'll call the police!" And again, the kind Mr. Webber called 9-1-1. Again, officers from the Brookline Police Department were at our door within minutes, and they helped me carry Gary down the stairs.

Gary was one of those children who had an unusually high threshold for pain, and he seldom cried when he was hurt. He was more sorry that he'd broken the French door than anything else, and he kept saying, "I'm sorry, Mom, for breaking the door!"

I wrapped tight the blood-soaked towels around his leg and kissed him over and over, saying, "Don't worry about it. You'll be all right, you'll be all right."

With my bleeding son in my arms, we sped through the streets of Boston with a siren blaring and blue lights flashing. Déjà vu?

At the Children's Hospital, a doctor sewed up Gary's foot with a dozen stitches and gave him a pair of crutches. I think he was a celebrity of a sort at school for a few weeks as he hopped around on his crutches.

My First Homecoming

In the summer of 1961, nine years after the American occupation of Japan ended, and the Korean conflict had helped to boost Japanese economy, my father was able to send me a round-trip plane ticket to

Japan. Earle was on a summer break, and our daughter Julie was twelve, old enough to look after her brothers. It had been thirteen years since I had seen my sisters and friends. Our promise that I would return to Japan in five years after I'd come to America had been postponed numerous times to enable Earle to get more education to help his future career. I had almost given up hope of ever seeing my beloved homeland. I was thirty-four years old, and this was my first plane trip. I tried to act nonchalant, but my heart was pumping fast as we took off from Boston's Logan airport. As the plane climbed to unimaginable heights, I saw the clouds below, and for the first time in my life, felt the presence of God.

As the plane landed at Haneda International Airport, the only major airport in Tokyo then, I pressed my forehead on the small window trying to see if I could find anyone I knew among the sea of people behind the fence. My heart began to beat fast with excitement. I saw my father waving his hand, and then my sisters, and then my dear friends, all shouting and calling me. The baggage checking and the customs seemed to take an eternity.

Finally released of all the necessary duties, I ran and jumped into my father's arms. *"Tadaima!"* I cried out, tears running down my face. *Otohsama!* (I'm home! Father!)

"Okaeri! Okaeri!" (Welcome home!)

My sisters and friends surrounded me and shouted, "You are home! You are home!" There was not a dry eye among them. Thirteen years is a long time.

My first homecoming was a dizzying whirlwind trip. My classmates arranged a special class reunion in my honor. There were numerous get-together parties with friends and relatives. My father planned an auto trip to the Hakone hot spring for me with my younger sister, Aiko, and Uta, our former governess, my father's concubine and second wife. My sister seemed to have found a working relationship with Uta. She seemed a little more settled, now that her position as a legitimate wife was secured. (In old Japan, it was a fairly common practice for wealthy men to have concubines.)

We went to nightclubs, my first such experience. We wined and dined at the best Tokyo could offer. Before the war, it was very rare for people to own automobiles. But now, my father had a brand new Toyota

Crown and a chauffeur. Department stores were stocked with expensive brand-name goods, and an army of smartly dressed elevator girls and escalator girls, without a hair out of place, bowed deeply, and with sweet lilting voices greeted us. *"Irasshai Mase."* (Thank you for coming).

There was no trace of the devastation of the war I had left behind thirteen years ago. Japan had recovered and was thriving. This was the Tokyo I remembered as a child. I felt as if I was in a time warp, like Rip Van Winkle. The experience was intoxicating. The mundane life of a thrifty housewife in America seemed so remote and far away. I felt a twinge of regret for the life I had left in Japan.

Dream House

After two years at Mrs. Levy's apartment, we happened to come upon a great find through our daughter's classmate. Her family was moving out of a big house next to a synagogue just across the street from Devotion School where our children attended. I found that the synagogue was the landlord, and for four hundred dollars a month, we could have a three-storied house with six bedrooms, two fireplaces, three full baths, a two-car garage, and a yard big enough to play badminton! This was truly a dream house.

A big cherry tree outside of our dining room gave us magnificent blossoms in the spring and bore cherries. We invited our friends and had cherry-picking parties. I made cherry pies and froze a dozen or so for winter months. A grapevine in the back gave us small but sweet green grapes.

The house was only minutes away from the trolley line and grocery stores. This house was truly a gift from heaven; it was a perfect place to raise a growing family. We shared the driveway with our landlord, a Jewish synagogue, and we would watch catering trucks roll in on weekends laden with food with wonderful aroma for bar mitzvahs and weddings. Our children learned about Jewish holidays and customs from many friends who attended the Hebrew school after regular school.

Arthur, the Traffic Cop

When our youngest son, Mark, started school, I met Arthur. He was a portly traffic cop with a friendly smile. He was at the school crossing in the morning and in the afternoon, giving words of encouragement to the kids. Arthur sometimes chastised them for their misbehavior, but the kids knew that they could always count on Arthur for help if they needed it. I would accompany Mark to and from school and chat with Arthur when he was not busy. Sometimes if he saw me waiting at the curb, he would stop the traffic for me to cross, wink at me and then say, "They are sitting. They can wait." Such flexibility was unbelievable in Japan where everything was done "by the book."

To me, Arthur epitomized what I thought of as a "good American." He was good-natured, had a wonderful sense of humor, and was always ready to extend a helping hand.

Barcus Youth Center

The location, size, and setup of our new house worked like a magnet for children. It was a great stop-off point after school for our children's friends. Also, the word got out that I baked bread and chocolate chip cookies.

Children spilled from every corner of the house and yard. They knew the house rules, though. I did not tolerate bad manners. Many years later I would run into some of the boys, now grown and fathers themselves, and we would reminisce about those "good old days" at 15 Williams Street, picking cherries and playing badminton or basketball by the garage.

The Beatles had ushered in the *Age of Aquarius*. Every teenage boy fancied himself a rock musician and dreamed of making it big. Gary was no exception. His "band" practiced in our basement once a week. On those days, I would fortify myself with a couple of aspirins and endure the noise that traveled from below and vibrated throughout the house. *Boom, boom, boom, boom* "yeah … yeah …" I could never quite make out the words, but the boys were earnest. When they finally surfaced with flushed and sweaty faces, a plate of chocolate chip cookies awaited them.

It was a time when public schools were rich in music and art. All of our children took free lessons, Julie in clarinet, Gary in trombone and tuba, and Mark in cornet. Julie and Gary were in the high school band and orchestra. Under the leadership of a fabulous music director, Mr. Madden, the band made all-state many times. Gary was so good that Mr. Madden even had a tuba solo for Gary in one of many Brookline High School concerts in the quadrangle. The high school band would come to our house for a backyard barbecue and badminton until the sun went down and swallowed us in the twilight.

Mark played in the grade school band at Devotion School. Earle dusted off his old trombone that he used to play in college and joined the Brookline town band. During the summer, they played outdoor concerts on top of the Larz Anderson Park overlooking the city of Boston with its skyline as a backdrop. In their spiffy uniforms, they marched the streets in Brookline on July 4 and Memorial Day. Our daughter fell in love with a brass player, a man with the bluest blue eyes I have ever seen.

In the meantime, Gary was turning into quite an athlete, receiving the Halpern Trophy at the high school for winning the pentathlon. He was on the track and wrestling teams. He made the football team his sophomore year. Under the tutelage of a great coach, Mr. Schluntz, by his junior year he was a celebrated running back. Since Julie was in the band and Gary was on the playing field, Earle, Mark, and I were in the cheering section for all of the home games. I got caught up in the energy, just as I had in 1948 when, only a few days after I arrived in America, I'd seen my very first football game in Champaign. I had absolutely no idea what was going on at first.

Once, I saw Gary running with the ball, and a swarm of hefty linebackers bulldozed over him. When the dust settled, I saw my son stretched out on the field not moving. I started to get up and run to him. Earle pulled my shirttail and stopped me. "They have people who take care of him. They don't want mothers out there," he said.

I sighed in relief when Gary got up and walked off the field under his own power. We even invited the entire football team to our house once, but football players are a breed apart. They ate and left.

Our life, it seemed, was moving along as I had dreamed. Earle was promoted to full professorship, and we were in love with Boston. I did not recognize the wind of imperceptible change in the air that would throw us into an uncharted sea, and ensuring that America would never be the same.

John F. Kennedy was elected president of the United States. For the first time in U.S. history, we had a royalty-caliber couple as the head of our nation. President Kennedy's beautiful wife, Jackie, set the fashion trend. I even made a pillbox hat and a short jacket suit for myself, wanting to emulate Jackie. She brought class to the White House. We simply adored this handsome couple and were so proud to have them represent our country.

On November 23, 1963, I was waiting for the trolley on Beacon Street on the way home from my part-time job at Boston University. Suddenly, a man ran out of the store screaming something. Then another man ran out crying and shouting. People around me looked at each other:

"What is he saying?"

"What happened?"

"I don't know."

Then we heard a passerby shout the news: "Kennedy has been assassinated!"

We were stunned. We couldn't believe these words. *Our prince cannot die!* Just as we heard these words, the trolley arrived. My fellow passengers and I got on the trolley, and some of the men repeated what we'd heard in loud voices: "President Kennedy has been assassinated!"

A gasp went through the trolley. "Oh no!" Some started to cry. My heart was beating so fast that I could hardly breathe. I jumped off at my stop, ran home, and turned on the TV. *No, no, this can't be true!* An almost hysterical announcer was giving a minute-by-minute account of what was going on in Texas. Yes, it was true that our beloved president had been shot to death as his motorcade wound through the streets in Houston. Pretty soon, the children returned home, and with tears in our eyes, we gathered in the TV room. Earle came home from work and joined us. I think we even ate our supper there that night, not wanting to miss a word. I felt as if a huge, dark cloud had covered the entire United States. The age of Camelot was over.

CHAPTER XII: Awakening

A New Era

Ever since I had met Betty, the crackerjack legal secretary, back in the '50s in Stadium Terrace, my idea *of shokugyou fujin* (working woman), which was scorned in Japan when I was growing up, was completely altered. I dreamed of someday becoming a self-assured secretary like her. In the 1950s most of us accepted the narrow definition of woman's life as homemaker, schoolteacher, nurse, or secretary. From what Betty told me, the life of a secretary was exciting, challenging, and glamorous. So when our youngest son began school, I enrolled in the two-year business program at Boston University where I learned how to manage an office, how to type on a manual typewriter, and take Gregg's shorthand. My first assignment after completing the program was to work part-time for the dean at the School of Management. This was the first time I had ever worked in an office of any kind and received a paycheck. I felt so grown up and independent.

"You can work part-time so long as you don't neglect your duty as wife and mother," Earle cautioned me, so that I won't get carried away with my newfound independence. This meant that I should have his breakfast ready; be home when the children came home from school; keep the house clean and in order; make sure that all his shirts were laundered, starched, and ironed (we never sent his shirts out); and have a decent meal on dinner table every night.

With my "own money," I opened my bank account. It was liberating not to have to go to Earle for five or ten dollars for every little thing. With my newfound financial freedom, I decided to pursue three things I loved: ballet, music, and art. Boston Ballet was just being formed under the leadership of Virginia Williams. I began attending the school's adult classes. It had been more than thirty years since I'd pirouetted or done a plié at the barre. I then signed up for free student tutoring for piano from a young graduate student at the School of Music at Boston University. I had not touched the piano since I'd left Earle's parents' home on Church Street in Champaign ten years before.

As if my creative energy that had been bottled up for so long was bursting forth, I also enrolled in the Museum of Fine Arts adult education classes to start from scratch in drawing, oil, and watercolor. I discovered that cultural differences were clearly reflected in art. While I was in my oil painting class, my teacher, Ms. Sears, would boom with her authoritative voice, "Cover the canvas! Make your statement! Don't be wishy-washy!" I also took up Japanese brush *sumi-e* painting class with Mr. Matsumoto. He would admonish us to "let the blank space speak." By not covering the entire paper, he said, and by leaving a large blank space, unspoken thoughts and feelings were embraced in it.

The juxtaposition of my two classes was truly a lesson in the cultural dichotomy of Japan and America. The Japanese approach of understatement, the cultural belief that less is better and harmony should be foremost at all cost versus the American approach of self-expression, abundance, and the bigger the better were clear in the two media. Oil painting demanded the "push and pull" of light and dark, expression of power, and the three-dimensionality of subjects, while the *sumi-e* painting was an expression of ethereal delicacy, with almost one-dimensional containment of Zen simplicity.

One day, Ms. Sears stopped by my easel and watched me in silence for a long time and said, "Faith, you paint with a Japanese approach. When you get these two approaches reconciled in your mind, you will become a good painter."

The Boston Museum of Fine Art had been a place of spiritual solace long before I began taking classes. When my youngest son was still a toddler, I had enrolled the older children in their Saturday classes, and used to wander around the museum with Mark in tow. I felt at home there. There was a small room solely devoted to Jean Francois Millet's work. I had always been drawn to his somber paintings, and the room became my spiritual haven. Whenever I was troubled, I would go there and find solace. When all of my children were in school, I began working mornings and going to classes in the afternoons, as if I were in a frenzy of capturing the lost time. I was playing Chopin again, drawing and painting, and pirouetting.

New Friend, New World

In the dean's office, I met a young woman who took an interest in Japanese culture. She wanted to know Japanese art. We decided to study Japanese brush painting together. Gee Gee was not only outspoken but also totally unconventional. Her father had abandoned the family when she was a little child, and her mother had put her and her sister in a convent to be brought up by the nuns.

When I visited her apartment, Gee Gee showed me her underwear and socks folded and arranged neatly in the drawers looking like marching soldiers, a habit she said she picked up at the convent. The flip side of her orderliness at home was her totally irreverent and impetuous behavior outside of her home. She taught me swearing words I'd never heard before. I was mesmerized by her spontaneous devil-may-care behavior.

She took me to a feminist meeting of a group called "Bread and Roses" in a church basement in Cambridge. I felt completely out of place and intimidated. I sat close to Gee Gee and listened to other women heatedly talk about male chauvinism. I didn't know what that was.

"Faith, you are too obedient to Earle," Gee Gee would say.

"No I'm not!" I would counter.

"Well, you are always doing things to please him while he is doing whatever pleases him!"

"But I want him to be happy," I would explain.

"How about you?" Gee Gee would ask. "Shouldn't you be happy too?"

"I don't think that's so important," I would answer. And she would go into a long lecture on the American pursuit of happiness for everyone.

In 1969, there was a period of frequent assaults on women on the streets of Boston at night, and women were banding together to demonstrate to awaken the police and local politicians, who women felt were not taking the matter seriously enough. Gee Gee asked me to join the "Take Back the Night" demonstration in Copley Square."

I told Earle. He looked surprised, but he did not stop me. That was one thing he never did. He never stopped me outright from doing what I believe in, although sometimes he would show his displeasure by his silence.

In Copley Square, Gee Gee and I joined the throng and shouted, "Take back the night! Take back the night!"

The new experience, to me, was frightening and liberating at the same time. I began reading Simone de Beauvoir's *The Second Sex*, while Gee Gee was drawn into the world of Zen through Japanese brush painting. We talked about the meaning of "nothingness" in Zen, the liberation of women, and our never-ending struggle with men. Although I could never subscribe to her bohemian life of seeming abandon, I watched her with wonderment. I loved the classic ballet of tutu's, pink toe shoes, and precision steps. She abhorred it as constricting and unnatural and preferred the free-flowing form of Isadora Duncan.

Fashion Model

Gee Gee was opening my eyes to a new world with all kinds of possibilities beyond my ordered small world. One day I saw an advertisement for a fashion modeling school near Coolidge Corner, only a five-minute walk from our house. Since my mother had spoiled us by outfitting her three daughters with beautiful dresses she designed and made, I had been fashion conscious. The world of fashion models seemed to me like a very glamorous world. I signed up for their six-month course. All the students were in their teens or early twenties except me. Until that time, the extent of my makeup was face powder and lipstick. I had never heard of eyeliners or shadows or mascara. For me it was like playing house when I was a small child when I would secretly "borrow" my mother's lipstick and high-heeled shoes and strut around. We learned to walk, turn, sit, and strike various poses with different styles of clothes.

For our graduation, we had a fashion show and dinner at a dinner theater called Monticello in Framingham. Each student was to model three outfits of her own. I designed and made a red velvet two-piece lounge wear, a Chinese-style Mandarin long gown in pink and gold brocade, and a rust-colored, knit gaucho outfit worn with boots and a wide-brimmed gaucho hat that was in vogue then. The school actually taught a special stance called the gaucho stance to model the gaucho outfit! I wore a beautiful gold pendant with a cameo, which Earle had given me for my first birthday after I'd come to America, and a large, jade ring my mother had given me when I left Japan.

The changing area was cramped, and we each secured a small space to run back and change into another outfit as music played on the stage. Sadly it was not until I returned home, that I discovered my pendant and ring had both been taken out of my jewelry box. This taught me a lesson: never wear good jewelry at fashion shows.

After "graduation," I modeled a few times at luncheon shows for a local dress store. Most places we went had no dressing room, and we had to change

139

our clothes in a makeshift corner in a storage closet. Over expense-account, two-martini lunches, smartly attired men would whisper lewd remarks as we walked the aisle. There was no glamour. Another lesson learned.

Gee Gee was now working as a fashion photographer for Jordan Marsh, a big department store in downtown Boston. She was delighted that I had learned to model and wanted to take my picture for her portfolio. We would go up to Mission Hill overlooking the city, a blue-collar section of Boston where she lived, and I had fun posing for her while the curious neighborhood boys stopped their play and watched.

Bowling Buddies, Drinking Buddies

Earle had never forgotten his working-class roots, and even after he became a professor at Boston University he continued to befriend service workers there. He joined the university bowling league, won many prizes, traveled out of state for tournaments, and enjoyed the camaraderie and carefree atmosphere of all-night poker games and drinking with his bowling buddies, without being rowdy or reckless as some of them were. His mother had told me that ever since he was a small child, Earle was never rowdy, even when he was in the midst of mischief. On his bowling tournament trips, I would often pack celery and carrot sticks in a plastic bag for him so that he won't be tempted by chips and other unhealthy snacks and send him off with a word of caution, "Don't drink too much!"

I was never fond of bowling, especially since I was not good at it. Moreover, I was not good drinking company. My drinking days in college were mostly on a dare and to be "cool," not because I was fond of alcohol, and I had stopped drinking after I started having children. I invited his bowling buddies and their wives for a buffet dinner, but the liquor flowed too freely, and once a man got too drunk and fell down the stairs, and another became so rowdy that the tradition was finally discontinued.

Earle had another circle of drinking buddies—his colleagues and teaching assistants at the university. It was almost a nightly ritual on weeknights after school for them to gather at Anita Chu's, a great watering hole-cum-Chinese restaurant in Coolidge Corner, for a few drinks and spareribs. This group seldom got rowdy, and we'd have them over at our house for dance parties. Just as my parents used to do when I was a little girl, we would push the dining table and chairs in the corner and turn our dining room into a mini ballroom. A couple of young faculty, teaching assistants, and some graduate students and their spouses would gather at our house and dance to the big band music or listen to the then wildly popular Beatles. I was not good company for drinking, but when it came to dance time, I was the life of a party, and my honey-garlic chicken wings were legendary.

Around the World in 21 Days

In December 1968, my father gave us our greatest Christmas present—five airline tickets to go around the world to destinations of our choice and ending in Tokyo. We decided that the following summer would be ideal, as Gary would be graduating from high school.

In July of 1969, with three children, twelve, eighteen and twenty, we visited England, Denmark, France, Switzerland, Greece, Jerusalem, India, Thailand, Cambodia, and Hong Kong in twenty-one days. It was a one-night stop in most places, except in France, where we drove from Paris in a rented Peugeot down the French countryside to the Pyrenees and to Geneva, Switzerland.

The reason we took time to see the French countryside, particularly the Pyrenees, was to visit the village where Earle's ancestors were believed to have come from. A few years back, Earle had received a picture postcard from one of his graduate students who was traveling in France. The postcard had a pastoral scene of southern France and the name "Barcus" splashed across it. The student wrote: "Thought you might be interested to know of a village with your name." It piqued our interest, and we wrote to the mayor of Barcus, France, not really expecting any kind of response. To our amazement, we received a lovely letter from Monsieur Jaughiverrey, the mayor of Barcus, inviting us to stop by during our trip in Europe. Luckily, our daughter had studied French and became our translator.

Barcus was a small village nestled in the rolling hills of the Pyrenees in southern France, with perhaps a population of a few hundred. An ox cart lumbered along the main street, and the mayor also ran the village's only general store. Besides the mayor's store, the main street consisted of a church, an inn, and a bakery. We stayed in the tiny inn with Spartan furnishings and had fried steaks and potatoes for dinner. The mayor invited us to his home for wine and cheese. The mayor's oldest daughter, Bernadette, had been studying English, hoping to visit America some day, and between our daughter's school French and Bernadette's "English," conversation flowed. The mayor told us that there had been a large migration of people from that area to the United States in the late nineteenth century. He also explained to us the origin of the name Barcus, pronounced bar-koos in French; it meant "a verdant valley." We began corresponding with the Jaughiverrey family after our trip, and the following summer, Bernadette came to stay with us for a month. Although we have lost touch now, we still enjoy a present they gave us—a specialty of that region, a large bright red–and–white-checkered tablecloth and matching napkins.

Laundry, and what to see, were the biggest challenges during our journey, as our children were spread out in ages and of both genders. I think our Julie had to suffer through the antics of her brothers. Earle and I had our handful trying to figure out flights, transportation, money, lodging, meals and *laundry*!

Gary had read about the amazing story of how Hong Kong tailors could make a man's suit in one day. Although we were in Hong Kong only two days and sick from the dinner the night before, he managed to have a tailor come to the hotel and measure him and had two beautifully tailored suits made in one day!

On July 20, 1969, we arrived in Tokyo, bedraggled and sick from unaccustomed food and exhaustion. The summer in Tokyo is like being in a steam bath. My father swept us away to his new home in Sanya, a suburb of Tokyo, where Uta and Aiko had prepared cold drinks and snacks. My father had built a sixteen-unit condominium building where his house used to be, and he lived on the first floor unit with a garden. He had saved a two-bedroom unit on the third floor for our use. It was tight for five of us, but we were happy to have free lodging.

Our youngest, Mark was so curious that he kept opening and closing the paper sliding doors that separated rooms and opened to the closets where Futon bedding were kept during the day. Our children got a kick out of taking off their shoes at the entrance and changing into cloth slippers and then removing those slippers when we entered the Japanese tatami rooms. Sometimes even I forgot to take off my shoes or slippers, and Uta or Aiko would yell in horror, "Your shoes!"

Our children loved stepping out into the garden, wearing special wooden garden clogs placed on a steppingstone right at the edge of the Japanese room without walls and with paper sliding doors. They click-clopped on stepping stones that wound around the garden. My father watched them, beaming.

"You have no wall," our sons said.

"Don't need a wall. We have a removable wall," my father said, and he showed them the wooden sliding doors kept in a storage closet at the end of the corridor and rolled them out to completely close the room to form a "wall."

"Wow, that's really neat!" exclaimed our boys.

I loved the airiness and openness and realized how much I had missed this organic structure of a Japanese house.

The day we arrived in Tokyo was the day the American astronauts were to land on the moon. My father weighed the historical significance of this event and the state of our health, which was not great, but he decided in favor of the moon landing, a once-in-a-lifetime, historical event over medical attention. My American family and Japanese family together held our breaths and watched on TV as Neil Armstrong walked on the moon. We clapped our hands and exchanged "Congratulations!" and "*Omedetou!*" The entire nation of Japan congratulated the United States and joined in the celebration.

By my father's "orders," we were swept away for a checkup to St. Luke's Hospital in downtown Tokyo, the hospital in whose chapel Earle and I were married in 1947. After the doctor gave us a clean bill of health, for an R & R, my father sent us to our summer home in Oiwake.

I shared my love of my childhood paradise with my children, picking wild flowers and chasing fireflies. Villagers came to see Miss Nobuko's American family. We climbed my beloved Mt. Asama together, just as I had done when I was a child. Julie stayed behind at our cottage in the woods to catch up on her letters to her boyfriend back in the States. Asama was still serene, gently puffing a wisp of purple smoke and watched us silently.

Our sons discovered that in Japan you could buy fireworks at the country store, and they decided to put on a fireworks show for their grandfather, who was to come up from Tokyo. They bought a mountain of fireworks of all types, and in our large front yard rigged strings and sticks. When the night fell, they were ready. My father relaxed on the veranda in his cotton Kimono, sipping cold beer and anxiously waited for the "show" to begin. Our caretaker's family had heard about the boys' plans and came to watch.

Gary and Mark ran back and forth with matches between sticks and strings, and suddenly the field was aglow with light and sparkles and crackling sounds. We all clapped our hands and shouted. My father lifted his beer and yelled, "Good job, boys!"

The caretaker woman said in wonderment, "American children are ingenious!"

Uncharted World

America was changing. The 1960s was the era of movements: civil rights, women's equality, sexual freedom, and experimentation with drugs. Our sons' hair began to grow longer, the first sign of things to come. We had always respected our children's privacy and felt we had taught them right and wrong, and it was up to them to chart their own lives according to the principles we planted in them. Youth rebellion against adult authority is a normal part of life at any age.

But the '60s' rebellion was different and profound. In universities across the nation, students were doing "sit-ins" demanding changes. Civil Rights workers were being murdered, women were demanding equal rights, children were running away from home and joining dubious cults, "swinging" couples were exchanging their spouses, and youths were getting high on LSD. It was a frightening time. It seemed that America was coming apart at the seams, and the adults were helpless to repair it. We were all swept into the immutable tsunami waves of social change and could barely stay afloat.

Our daughter dropped out of college and went off to Nantucket with her blue-eyed boyfriend one summer to work at Sears Roebuck. We picked up our son Gary at the police station for riding his friend's motorcycle without a license. He wanted a motorcycle in the worst way, but we held our line as we felt motorcycle accidents were too often fatal. We finally reached a compromise and bought him a used car. He went off to Canada with a friend, and on the way home slipped on an icy road, flipping the car. He came home alive with only cuts and bruises and a few dents on the car.

Even our youngest, the darling of teachers in grade school, now struggled to stay in high school. I became very sensitive to the strangely sweet smell that sometimes wafted out of our son's room. I was going through my own midlife crisis. I set up an easel in my room and tried to find my equilibrium in art. Earle was fully occupied as before with his work, golf, bowling, band, and going out with the "boys." It seemed as if we had lost our mooring and everyone in the family was scattering in every direction.

Awakening

The family trip to Japan had sounded an alarm in my mind. There were so many facets of Japanese culture that I had forgotten. For twenty years I had been so busy learning the American way that I had neglected my own roots.

I immersed myself for two years in relearning my own culture, reading book after book about Japan, its history, religion, education, art, and social customs, and I wrote and illustrated in pen and ink a book called: *An Illustrated Book of Japan in a Nutshell.* It was not a scholarly treatise but an easy-to-read overview of Japanese culture, moral values, customs, religious traditions, and school system, designed to give the first-time traveler to Japan a nutshell understanding of Japan and its people. Although it was seriously considered for publication by the Charles E. Tuttle Company of Vermont, the published version never materialized. Writing this book was cathartic for me, as I honored my native culture by expressing in writing what I cherished.

As for my personal interest in art, I had never quite mastered the oils, an aggressive medium, and moved on to drawing, watercolor, woodcut, and etching. I joined a local art society and exhibited in their group shows, won awards in their juried shows, and later was made a member of Copley Society of Artists. A small gallery in Brookline sponsored my work, and I sold paintings and etching prints. I had a couple of one-person shows. After trying various art media for nearly ten years, the exacting nature of etching held my interest the longest. I felt I needed my own etching studio to work freely. By then, our children had grown, I had a full-time job at a publishing company in town, and Earle and I had moved out of our big "dream house" to a two-bedroom condominium.

Through a friend, I found an elderly couple who would love to rent their basement as my studio. It was only a five-minute walk from my home. Through my art teacher, I ordered a custom-made, manually operated etching press. This was the first time I had "set up shop" of my own. Although Earle fiercely believed in everyone's individual rights to do what he or she wanted to do and that others should not interfere, at first he was not happy about me setting up shop on my own. Eventually, though, he came around.

"In America"

Earle's mother passed away in 1975, but my father-in-law continued to live in their house alone, cherishing his independence. After a few years, he had a widow friend. One summer they came to Boston for a sightseeing trip and stayed with us. They were pleasantly surprised that there were lots of trees in Boston, and it was not an asphalt jungle as they had imagined.

Along with the women's movement and other movements of the '70s was the health movement, and we were all learning (for me relearning) the virtue of tofu and stir-fries. When I was in Illinois, we cooked everything to death. Now we prized the tender crisp of stir-fry. One evening, I served stir-fried green beans.

My father-in-law said, "Hey, these green beans aren't cooked."

I explained to him that you get more nutrients that way. He saw chopped scallions on the salad and asked me what it was.

I said, "It's scallions, Daddy."

"What's a scallion?"

At this point, his lady friend said, "Dear, *in America* we call it green onions."

The only people who realized the significance of what she said were Earle and I. To them, *Boston was not quite America.*

Rebirth

My friend, Gee Gee, had moved on, marrying an Israeli sailor whom she had known for five days. But her legacy lived on. I had been plagued on and off with a back problem that started with my first pregnancy twenty-six years before and also developed various chronic allergies, sinus headaches, gastritis, insomnia, constipation, and bronchial illnesses. I was just beginning to find my own life apart from that of wife and mother. I realized that if I were to live my life to the fullest, I must be healthy.

I began reading book after book about illness and healing. *The Body in Question*, by Dr. Jonathan Miller, had taught me how the body works. Through *Medical Mystery*, by Dr. Steven Jonas, I learned that doctors don't always have all the answers, or even the right answers. In *Mental and Elemental Nutrients*, by Dr. Carl Pheiffer, I learned how each nutrient you take in your body works to keep you well. Dr. Ronald Glasser's *The Body is the Hero* taught me the wisdom and power of the body to heal. Dr. Hans Selye's books taught me the mind/body connection to illness. I read dozens of books, including Adelle Davis's, about how our lifestyle affected our health. I began to wean myself from potentially harmful foods, such as too many sweets, fried foods, cola drinks, and red meats. My back problem had flared up from time to time, and at one point it got so bad that I could hardly walk. I went to a famed orthopedic surgeon, and he said it was a pinched nerve and recommended a painkilling drug and a corset. The drug turned me into a "zombie," and without it, the pain was unbearable.

I had read about successful treatments of acupuncture in an alternative newspaper. It would be decades before the treatment was recognized as a thousand-year-old, legitimate cure for certain illnesses. I remembered seeing a sign in the window of a Chinese acupuncture office down the street not far from our home. Desperate for the first time in my life, I decided to give it a try. Timidly I hobbled into the office. I lay on my stomach and felt a little prickling sensations as the Chinese acupuncturist inserted thin needles on my lower back. My back pain was so great that these little pin pricks seemed like nothing. I lay there looking like a pin cushion and soon fell asleep. A half hour later, the assistant awoke me and told me, "You can get up now."

I looked at her doubtfully, and she just smiled back. To my amazement, I *could* stand up straight! I think I only paid twenty-five dollars. When I *walked* out of the acupuncturist's office without pain, I became a believer in alternative medicine.

I had read in the newspaper that the National Organization of Women recommended martial arts as a good assertiveness training for women. I wondered if my back could take the rigorous workout of martial art. I decided that it would either "kill me or cure me" and signed up for an Okinawan karate school on Columbus Road in downtown. The neighborhood was not particularly safe, and the teacher came to class with liquor on his breath. After a few months, I left him, and enrolled in Korean karate, called tae kwon do. The teacher seemed more interested in making money than teaching. I was becoming disillusioned in the world of martial arts.

One night, I went to see a martial arts demonstration at the old John Hancock Hall in town. I was particularly impressed with a demonstration by a young Korean instructor and his students. There was something that was very calm and refined about his demeanor. He didn't have that macho swagger that you sometimes see in men of martial arts. He was slim and small, yet his kicks were so powerful that he shattered with ease two boards held together by his students.

I enrolled in Mr. Jae Kim's tae kwon do school over a diner near Kenmore Square. I was forty-eight years old. Amazingly, my back held up. In fact, the rigorous workout seemed to dissipate the tension from my back, which was the root cause of my back problem. I was surprised to meet such a slender young man who was a graduate student at Harvard Business School as the master martial artist. Mr. Kim came from a privileged background of a Korean diplomatic family. He spoke flawless English, and had impeccable manners.

learning

Is This All There Is?

A 52-year-old "housewife and mother" asked herself that question and finally came up with a resounding, "No!"

by Faith N. Barcus

I'm probably the only 52-year-old woman who studies Martial Arts. It may even seem crazy to some people, but all I know is that in the four years I've been taking Tae Kwon Do (a Korean Martial Art), I have gotten a kind of mental and physical stability that I never had before.

My husband, who used to be completely put off by the whole idea of his wife taking up such a "masculine activity," now encourages me. He's seen what it's done for me, particularly in ways which consequently affect him.

Many people now ask me how I stay so healthy or where I get my energy. My answer is, "I work at it." I do. I know so I am not one of those genetically lucky people who are born with "Mack truck" type durability.

Unresolved tension and anger were draining me and actually making me ill. After 20-odd years of marriage and three children, I woke up one morning and said to myself, "Who am I? What am I doing? Where am I going?"

The only answer I could come up with was, "I'm a wife and mother." That that only said a part of me — not the whole of me, and I really didn't know where the rest of me had gone.

I used to have fairly clear edges, but over the years, playing the mother and wife roles had made those edges fuzzy. Being a wife and mother was what I did best, my husband would assure me. My mother-in-law agreed.

Yet, somewhere inside, the question kept gnawing at me: "Is this all there is to life?" Little by little the question surfaced, and with it came turbulent side effects in my relationship with my husband and children.

That was more than five years ago. In those five years I thought a lot about a married woman's life. I thought about my own mother's life, my mother-in-law's life, and the lives of all the married women I have known intimately.

I devoured book after book about women written by women. Whenever I could, I talked with other married women, not about children or recipes, but about their feelings and needs. The picture was pretty grim.

Since then, I've been climbing slowly and painfully from the pit of hopelessness to a rediscovery of myself.

An important part of that climb was my decision to take up one of the Martial Arts. I had been taking ballet lessons for several years (an acceptable "feminine" activity) and was always fascinated by Martial Arts, but never had the nerve to try it. Since I was stirring up 20-odd years of status quo and plunging my family into confusion by doing the unexpected, one more unorthodoxy didn't matter, I reasoned.

It turned out to be one of the best things I could have done for myself. Strong competitive sports are supposed to be a good way to get rid of tension and stress, but if you don't like to lose, or if you are the type who takes these things seriously, losing can just add to your frustration. I found that in the day-to-day rigorous workout in martial arts, these strong feelings are effectively resolved by kicking and hitting an imaginary opponent.

After a few months of kicking and hitting someone who once unconsciously I have suffered for 20 or more years began to disappear. And there were other benefits. I became less tired. I developed more zest for life, and the self confidence I was looking for came almost automatically.

After a hard day at the office, I'm so tired that even my vision is affected — the world becomes a blur. I fall asleep on the MTA. I'm tempted to head straight home and flop down into bed, but I force myself to go to my Tae Kwon Do class. I'm never disappointed.

After one hour of workout, all the tension in my body is completely dissipated. My head becomes clear, and I can actually see better (my opthalmologist didn't believe me) and that big pain of "rock" in the back of my neck is gone. I am full of energy and can spend a productive evening.

Once I saw what Tae Kwon Do did for me, I began to talk to other women in the school to see if they had gotten as much from the Martial Arts training as I had.

When I found that they had, another woman, an MIT graduate student, and I decided to do a study of the psychological and physical benefits of the Martial Arts training for women. We contacted all the Martial Arts schools in Boston that had women students and sent a questionnaire to them that we developed with the help of a professional researcher.

Most women, we have found, first get into one form of Martial Arts or another for self defense. But once they start, they are surprised to find that there is a lot more to Martial Arts than just self defense. They find that it's a total mind/body conditioning, which gives them the kind of self confidence they haven't been able to find through other physical exercise.

Several women said they took up martial arts after their friends had been raped or robbed. Joan, a graduate student in Sociology, used to live next to a park, a hang-out for teenage gangs, where one woman had been raped. Joan was also harassed by the gang, and one night was attacked and knocked down by three or four boys while a dozen or so men and women watched without helping.

Although Joan was not raped or critically injured, she realized that she couldn't depend on others to help her in time of crisis. She had only a few choices. She could stay at home at night. She could make sure she was with several people at all times, or with a mate (which was very impractical), or she could learn to fight fire with fire. So she took up the Ueshi kyu style of Martial Arts.

"It's fine to talk about taking control of one's life as a person and a woman," she says, "and this can be done to a certain extent analytically and intellectually, but I question how a woman can possibly talk about this in any meaningful sense when her very existence as a physical being is under constant threat. Unless I can be in control of my own body as much as possible, this belief in woman's independence is nothing but an intellectual word game without substance."

"In our society, we're taught to always be 'nice.' Yet we live in a society where things are happening fast and furiously. And we are exposed to constant stress, tension, anxiety and frustration just from the normal day-to-day living, not to mention other fearful events such as nuclear threat and the increasing number of street crimes."

We women are particularly vulnerable. We have been taught to be 'nice' little girls, so what do we do with those strong human emotions? Most of us keep them bottled up inside. There are not many legitimate outlets for our hidden anger and anxiety. Even with the women's movement, it is still frowned upon for a woman to show any aggressive feelings — malicious gossip and tongue lashing because these things are not visibly aggressive behavior used to punching somebody in the mouth. They are pay for being 'nice' — suppressed anger, frustration, and other strong feelings — often shows up as ulcers and other stomach disorders, migraine headaches, back aches, and the like.

Drug addiction, including the socially accepted 'pill popping' — valium, librium, other tranquilizers, sleeping pills, even aspirin — alcoholism, compulsive eating, smoking and other self-destructive things we do to ourselves, are almost always rooted in unresolved anger, frustration and fears.

Many women who have been taught to be 'nice' all of their lives don't even realize that they have aggressive feelings. Dr. Alexander Lowen at the Essen Institute points out:

Behind an attitude of submission, one always finds a layer of defiance and rebellion associated with suppressed negative and hostile feelings... In adults the submissive attitude is a defense against inner feelings of rebellion and hostility...

How many submissive women do you know? The word 'aggressive' in most people's minds conjures up all kinds of bad images, such as being 'pushy' or violent. And that's what happens to aggressive feelings when they're expressed through negative channels. When they are expressed in a healthy way, they serve a valuable self-preservative function.

Another aspect of Martial Arts training which many women mentioned was the ability to 'focus.' Peggy, a young tennis organizer, says, "When I learned this total body/mind focus, I suddenly found myself doing all kinds of things I thought I couldn't do before. I've gained self-confidence and inner strength. There was a gradual change of attitude to a more positive one. I began to feel a sense of pride in myself."

Women of all walks of life seem to take up Martial Arts. The benefits they get and the feats at total mind/body conditioning. Most women I interviewed expressed doubts as to whether they could have handled them develop mental and physical alertness.

Many women expressed this feeling of being in control of their own bodies as an important aspect of having confidence in themselves.

I liked the structured and respectful environment without militant directives. The fact that there were many women and children in his school also encouraged me. This was not a macho school. After work, I would attend his class two or three nights a week, and as weeks and months went by, I could feel the gradual transformation in me. Through punching and kicking invisible opponents, and loudly yelling, "Yah!" from the depth of my belly, the tension began to dissipate from my neck and shoulder—an ongoing condition I had had since I'd immigrated to America.

I began to have more energy. As I was promoted to higher ranks, self-confidence came as a byproduct of improved technique. Even after an especially busy day at work, when my body said, "go home and relax," I would force myself to get off the train at Kenmore station to attend Mr. Kim's class. I was never disappointed. After one hour of rigorous workout, I was totally energized.

When I first faced a man in practice sparring, my knees trembled and my stomach was in a tight knot. I had always been interested in kendo, a Japanese sword martial art because of our samurai ancestors, but actually sparring with a man a head taller than me was entirely a new and foreign world to me. It was not as serious as the real competition, but I remember a lot of adrenaline flowed through my body. I had been taking ballet, and I was limber and nimble, but I was still not confident of my power. Mr. Kim did not encourage stunts like breaking boards in his school. He said it was for a show. One day, I was lamenting my lack of power in my punches and kicks, and he said casually, "You could break a board if you wanted to. It has nothing to do with how much muscle power you have."

"Oh, no, I could never break a board!" I assured him.

One night after a workout, Mr. Kim brought out a pine board and called two hefty male students to hold it. "Tell yourself, I can do it!" he instructed. "And focus all of your attention on your hand." He explained that it was the speed and focus that would make it possible to break the board.

I went through the motion several times to get the timing and focus together, and with a loud yell from the bottom of my belly, hit the board, breaking it in two! I stood there for a second, stunned, not believing my eyes. When I realized what I had done, I yelled "I did it!" I gave Mr. Kim a big hug.

He smiled and said, "I told you so."

That was the only time I saw him allow board breaking in school in the seven years I studied in his school. He had shown me then and there the power of a focused mind.

I did not progress as quickly as the teenagers, but little by little, I learned to block a punch, dodge a kick, and move quickly side to side and backward and forward. What I learned was to look at the opponent's eyes with such focus that you could almost anticipate what he was going to do. I miscalculated once when I was sparring with a higher-ranking man, and walked right into his kick and suffered a hair fracture on my rib. I did not attend class for three months. I didn't miss a day of work, although my ribs hurt every time I took a deep breath or bent over. But such injuries were rare, and as I learned more intricate maneuvers, my confidence grew.

For a privileged young man, Mr. Kim was exceptionally thoughtful of and sensitive to social injustices in the world. Through martial arts training, he had helped many kids from the ghetto to finish school and remake themselves into responsible men. I saw a black youth with severe diabetes who had been hospitalized for seizures turn into a healthy young man. A skinny and small white youth full of rage was transformed into a thoughtful young man who went to a community college, got a job, married, and settled down. For the first time in my life, I became friends with black people from the ghetto and lesbian women at Mr. Kim's martial art school.

He was very understanding and supportive of women and encouraged us to aggressively participate in competitions. When I was fifty-two and held a green belt ranking, he suggested I take part in the martial arts tournament at Madison Square Garden. He said he could sign me up in the "senior" division. After class one night, about a dozen of the chosen students in our school piled into three cars and drove to New York. I don't think Earle was too pleased, but I was not deterred. The two black belt women, Connie and Kay, and I shared a room at the YWCA. I was so excited and worried about the tournament the next day, I could not sleep a wink. There were all kinds of martial arts: Japanese karate, aikido, judo, jujitsu, Korean tae kwon do, Chinese kung fu, sword fighting, and forms I had never heard of.

The Madison Square Garden was packed, and I could feel the energy. The two women and I attended each other's event to give moral support, as the men were scattered in other areas. Once in a while, somebody would come running to tell us that so-and-so had just won the sparring. I saw some men get bloody noses. Mr. Kim had signed me up for the form competition rather than sparring. I didn't win anything, but the experience left an indelible memory in my mind.

One Sunday afternoon, I went to the school to work out. There was only one assistant instructor who was "minding the store," taking a nap on the couch. I changed into a uniform and began working out, punching and kicking the eighty-pound bag. I saw something move behind me, and when I turned around, I saw a tall dark figure disappear into the women's dressing room. "Hello!" I called.

No answer.

I quietly approached our dressing room. When I quickly pulled the curtain, I came face-to-face with a young black man about a foot taller than me. "What are you doing?" I exclaimed.

He mumbled something and held his jacket tight in front of him.

"What do you have there?" I grabbed his jacket collar and shook, and my wallet dropped out on to the floor.

By this time, the assistant instructor was awakened by the commotion and was standing right behind me. We chastised the young man and let him go.

Mr. Kim never encouraged this sort of confrontation. He used to say jokingly, "If you train hard in tae kwon do, you'd be in such good shape that you could always outrun the attacker. Don't be foolish and fight against knives and guns."

At the tae kwon do school, I became good friends with Allyson, a graduate student at Massachusetts Institute of Technology. We talked about the benefits of tae kwon do in our lives, and wondered if other women felt the same way. We decided to conduct a survey. With the help of Earle, whose expertise was research, we developed a questionnaire and distributed it to women students in all the martial arts schools in Boston. We found that most women started martial arts for self-defense, but once they started, they were surprised to find that there is a lot more

Faith Nobuko Araki Barcus

to martial arts than just self-defense. They find that it is a total mind/body conditioning, which gives them the kind of self-confidence they have not been able to achieve through other physical exercise.

Several women said they took up martial arts after their friends had been raped or robbed. Joan, a graduate student in sociology, used to live next to a park, a hangout for teenage gangs, where one woman had been raped. The gang often harassed Joan, and three or four boys knocked her down one night while a dozen men and women watched without helping. She realized that she couldn't depend on others to help her in time of crisis. She could stay at home at night, or make sure that when she went out she was with several people or with a male, which was not practical. So, she took up Uechi-ryu karate. She wrote on the questionnaire:

> It's fine to talk about taking control of one's life as a person and woman, and this can be done to a certain extent analytically and intellectually, but I question how a woman can possibly talk about this in any meaningful sense when her very existence as a physical being is under constant threat. Unless I can be in control of my own body as much as possible, this belief in woman's independence is nothing but an intellectual word game without substance.

Alexander Lowen of the Esalen Institute said:

> Behind an attitude of submission one always finds a layer of defiance and rebellion associated with suppressed negative and hostile feelings … In adults the submissive attitude is a defense against inner feelings of rebellion and hostility …

Another thing we learned from our survey was that women who had been studying martial arts for a year or more had gained the ability to focus. A young tenant organizer, Peggy, wrote:

> I learned this total body/mind focus, and suddenly I found myself doing all kinds of things I thought I couldn't do before. I've gained self-confidence and inner strength.

Pretty soon, I became addicted to the endorphin "high" I experienced after a workout. I started attending the class five nights a week and sometimes would go to work out on Sundays. My promotion was slow, but after seven years, I finally attained the rank of red belt, a rank below the black belt.

Before I was married, I thought I had fairly clear edges, but over the years playing the mother and wife roles had made those edges fuzzy. When I started martial arts, Earle seemed to be put off by my taking up such an aggressive, unladylike activity, but I was determined to continue. Gradually he saw the health benefit to me and came to accept my unorthodox health-promoting regimen. My article "Is This All There Is?" was about how Tae Kwon Do helped me to become totally healthy; it was published in the *Equal Times,* a feminist newspaper,

I gained the ability to focus, as so many women had reported in our survey. One by one, all of my health problems began to disappear. My disabling back problems disappeared. My lifelong sinus headaches were gone. I no longer had to depend on Gelusil tablets to quiet my stomach.

I was reborn.

CHAPTER XIII: BUILDING THE BRIDGE

My Father, the Charmer

My father remained an active participant as a pioneer in the world of management in Japan, even after he "retired." The emperor had decorated him with a *Ranju Houshou* (outstanding accomplishment) medal in 1960 and, in 1966, had given him *Kun Santo* (the Third Order of Merit) for his untiring work in improving Japan's productivity through efficiency management. In 1974, at age 79, my father received *Kun Nito* (the Second Order of Merit), the highest honor for ordinary citizens.

In 1975, when he was eighty years old, he led a group of Japanese Rotarians on an around-the-world trip. He left his group in New York for a few days and came to see me in Boston. I took a few days off from work and went to pick him up at Logan Airport.

"You look amazingly well, father!" I exclaimed as I wrapped my arms around him.

He beamed rather proudly and winked, an endearing habit of his, and said, "I'm not ready to go yet!"

I was truly amazed that he could walk so surefooted without help.

He had suffered a stroke five years ago and had lost his speech and use of his hand, but he had completely recovered. I took him to my workplace, a large publishing company in downtown, and as usual, he immediately captured everyone's heart. We gave a reception at our home, inviting Earle's colleagues and my friends at work, and again he was the center of discussion and charmed them all.

He was asked to be a featured speaker at the Brookline Rotary Club. Although he had won many debates in his youth, I was not quite sure of his English skills as a featured speaker, after so many years out of practice, and asked if they would make an exception to a men-only meeting and allow me to attend as his interpreter. My request was granted, and I accompanied my father.

He was in his element, talking about the economic trends in Japan and the world, spreading maps and charts on the wall. After his talk, one man raised his hand and said, "Mr. Araki, what do you think is the best stock to buy in Japan now?"

He smiled broadly and said, "Ah, you must be Jewish! Jewish people are always interested in making money!"

The audience burst into loud laughter, and I turned red, looking for some place to hide. Brookline is a town with a large Jewish population. From his demeanor, though, everyone knew that my father meant no malice or prejudice, and he had the time of his life talking to everyone, sharing his knowledge and forecasting the future of Japan.

Efficient Death

Every New Year's holiday, my father had a ritual of planning his funeral. His friends and colleagues thought it was a rather morbid custom, but his philosophy was based on efficiency. When the head of the family dies, the family is thrown into chaos and confusion, and it behooves any thoughtful head of the family to plan his funeral down to the minutest detail to avoid unnecessary worry and time, he said. Every New Year's day, he even composed the death poem , a long-held samurai ritual. He planned where and how the wake was to be held, the placement of his coffin, and how much dry ice needed to be put in the coffin. He calculated how many people would attend, noted where the funeral was to be performed, and even planned the dinner menu for the guests. Aiko, who was involved in his annual planning, said there was no sense of sadness about death in his planning. He planned as if he were building a new factory. He included in his guest list his barber and the head fireman in the neighborhood he had befriended. He was an egalitarian till the end. He had a ritual of checking into St. Luke's Hospital in Tokyo every year for a complete physical checkup.

On May 15, 1977, I received a call from Keiko.

"I have sad news for you." She paused. "Father died this morning at St. Luke's Hospital while he was there for an annual checkup."

"What! I didn't know he was sick. Nobody told me!" I cried out.

"No, he wasn't sick at all. He had a cold, but it happened to be his annual checkup time, so he admitted himself to St. Luke's Hospital as he has done every year for the past twenty years. They found him dead in his sleep. He went so peacefully with no sign of struggle or pain. It was very strange," she faltered, "as if he had planned this."

I said with tearful voice, "Isn't it just like Father? He even died efficiently."

"Yes, we are saying the same thing here," Keiko agreed. "No one expected it."

After I put the phone down, I closed my eyes, and an image of my father's smiling face with his famous wink filled my head. It was as if he was saying, "Nothing to be sad about. Everything is going according to my plan."

Everything *did* go according to his plan, including the number of people who attended his funeral. It was a magnificent funeral at the Aoyama Funeral Hall, presided over by eleven Buddhist priests and attended by well over a thousand people, from top government officials to the lowly neighborhood barber in a rented mourning frock.

My father's death reminded me that I had unfinished business. I left the publishing company and went back to school at Boston University to complete the education I had abandoned more than thirty years ago. I switched my major to management, and just as I had finished the program, another adventure awaited me.

One day, my next-door neighbor, Bertha, stopped me and asked, "Faith, there is this Japanese woman who is married to a friend of ours, and she is very, very homesick. She doesn't know any other Japanese. Do you think you could go over and talk with her and comfort her?"

"Sure, where does she live?" I asked. "And what does she do?" All my life I'd had a soft spot for the downtrodden and the unfortunate.

Bertha told me, "Her name is Shizu, and she's married to an American poet. They run a Japanese restaurant downtown, but I think she's had a nervous breakdown."

The next day, I made some Japanese snacks and went to call on Shizu.

Shizu was a sallow-complexioned, tiny, middle-aged woman, who stood barely five feet tall. Her long, disheveled, graying hair was carelessly rolled up in a loose bun on the back and held together with a pencil. Her eyes had dark circles underneath them and were swollen from crying. I gave her the snack I'd brought and made some Japanese tea for both of us in her cramped and littered kitchen. Our talk started slow, interrupted by many long silences and more crying. Slowly she opened up to me and between sobbing and wiping her tears. She mumbled, "Nobuko-san, I really don't like America."

"What is it that you don't like?" I said as softly as I could.

"People are rude," she answered.

"Well, yes they seem rude compared to the Japanese way because Americans are so straightforward," I tried to explain.

"When I married Eddie-san, I had no intention of coming to America. I thought we would live in Japan..." She began to sob again.

I put my arm around her shoulder and lifted her hair out of her eyes. "Oh, I'm so sorry to hear that. No wonder you are so unhappy," I consoled her. "So, how did you end up running a restaurant on Newbury Street if you didn't like America?"

She told me between sobs that she had met and married an American in Japan, and they had returned to his native Boston. It was not very clear to me why they'd had to return, but I did not press. She said she could not adjust to the new world. She simply did not like American life and culture and wanted to go home. Since she had run an ice-cream shop in Japan, her husband thought that, if he could get her involved in an ice-cream shop, she would overcome her longing for her home in Japan. So they'd borrowed money and started an ice-cream shop on Newbury Street, the Fifth Avenue of Boston.

I sensed that this was a case of major misjudgment on her husband's part and noncommunication on Shizu's part. Being Japanese, she probably did not clearly voice her feelings, and her husband had tried to "read" her mind from an American—male(!)—perspective.

Shizu's English skill was marginal, and so was her skill at running a business in America. The rent on Newbury Street was so high that they would need to sell a thousand orders of ice cream a day, seven days a week, just to meet the expenses. The winter had come, and ice-cream sales had dropped precipitously. She and her husband had decided to change the ice-cream shop to a Japanese restaurant, since Shizu was an excellent cook.

They'd borrowed more money, and spent a lot of money for an authentic decor and *handmade* plates. They wanted the Japanese ambiance and aesthetic. The name, Kaiseki, itself, meant formal tea ceremony meal, suggesting elegance and class. The poor woman was in the kitchen practically all day, every day, without an opportunity to learn about America, improve her English, or have any kind of fun. It was as if she were the gerbil in the cage, running, running, but never getting anywhere. Her husband was useless. He could not even tend the register. She'd had a nervous breakdown and had become almost catatonic, refusing to eat or speak. That is when my neighbor, a friend of Shizu's husband, had come to me.

I visited her several times, taking some Japanese snacks each time, and coaxing her to eat. She began to feel comfortable with me. One day she asked me if I would manage the restaurant while she went back to Japan and recuperated. I have inherited my father's *"Edokko"* streak, a true Tokyoite character that can never say "no" when asked for help. I had never run a restaurant. I didn't even know how to cook Japanese food! But seeing this pitiful woman before me, I simply could not say no.

A week later, the chairman of the board of trustees for the restaurant, a Harvard-educated CPA and a friend of Shizu's husband, came calling at my house. He grilled me, "What do you know about payroll?"

I answered what I remembered in my accounting class, although I had never actually done payroll.

"How would you handle inventory?"

Again, since I had no actual experience, I had to reach into what I'd learned in class and bluffed, "Oh, I would definitely follow FIFO (first in, first out)."

"Hmmm, how would you increase the business?"

"Well, there are a number of ways to do this. Name recognition is important. But in restaurant business, the word-of-mouth advertisement is the best way. We have to put out a product that people talk about and want to come back for more." I had read about these strategies in my case studies classes, but I had no idea whether they would in actuality work.

I'm sure the chairman was not fooled by my bluffing. Maybe he liked my spunk or he was desperate, because he formally asked me to take over the operation of the restaurant. We signed some legal papers.

When I look back, I'm amazed at my audacity. I was naive not to have looked into the financial situation of the restaurant. When I took over the operation, I was astonished to find that the restaurant was deep in debt in back taxes to both the federal and state governments. How to increase sales became my consuming goal.

I had never worked as hard as I did in running Kaiseki. It became a kind of mission for me. I wanted to keep the restaurant open until Shizu returned. I even came to enjoy that adrenaline rush before the store opened each night, as I inspected to make sure everyone and everything was in place. Once, I even donned the kimono that had been stored in the trunk in the attic for decades, to appear on the local evening TV show called *Look* to demonstrate "A Meal of the Day." I had been learning from the chief chef how to cook all the dishes our restaurant offered, and I decided on "Tori-no-sakamushi," chicken steamed in sake, as the feature dish for the TV show. Actually, the TV station wanted our chef to demonstrate, but he did not speak English, and I did not wish to miss this golden opportunity to promote our restaurant. I offered to do it.

Being not accustomed to the traditional attire, it took me about two hours to get my kimono on and tie the heavy and long sash. The day of shooting was a gray, rainy day. There I was in the pouring rain, in an expensive, hand-painted silk kimono my mother had given me, holding an umbrella, and hitching the kimono up so the bottom part would not get soiled. With my chef in tow, juggling plates and bags of ingredients and utensils, I arrived at Channel 7 studio in downtown Boston. I think my chef was more nervous than I was as he watched me from the side, making sure I didn't screw up any of the steps.

A tall, handsome young man, named, I think, Mr. Prince, was the program MC. The problem was that this was not a "Julia Child's Kitchen." It was an electric kitchen! In the short time segment, water refused to boil quickly, but I had to go on pretending the water was boiling. We did bring the finished product for the final view. I didn't realize until I got home and watched the taped video of the show that I had made a mistake in the recipe proportions while converting it from the restaurant's massive servings to smaller servings! I hope no one tried that recipe!

Chefs are artisans and tend to be temperamental. One night, I had an argument with the restaurant's chef over presentation of the food, and he walked out on me in the middle of a dinner rush. I took over the kitchen and fed eighty customers that night. In the steamy kitchen, my glasses kept slipping down my nose as I tried to read the orders that lined up on the little pegs in front of me. As I wiped sweat off my face with my sleeve, my mind was racing with the speed of lightning, switching from teriyaki recipe to tempura recipe and on to something else. I probably lost five pounds that night.

The worst thing about running a restaurant was my late nights. By the time I'd closed the restaurant, fed the employees, counted the money, and checked on the supplies for the next day, it was one or two in the morning. I enlisted Mark to help me out.

One day, the chairman of the board called me. "Congratulations, Faith!"

"Why?" I asked. "What did I do?"

"Did you know that Kaiseki was the only Japanese restaurant in Boston to make the Fodor's list?"

I could not believe it, but it was true. We continued to make the Fodor's list the following year. But Shizu never returned to America. In 1985, the restaurant was sold.

Marriage is like a House

Marriage is like a house. If it is to last, it needs constant care and attention. A leak in the ceiling or a crack in the window must be repaired right away, or the house will soon be beyond repair. My immersion in the restaurant business had caused a crack in Earle and my marriage. I was so absorbed in the business that we hardly saw each other. I would prepare his dinner and leave home when he returned from work and often would return after he had gone to bed. About this time, Earle was experiencing a burnout at work after twenty-five years at the university, but I did not recognize it. He went into depression. We had been married for thirty-eight years, and whenever I did not spend enough time with him, our marriage suffered. I should have learned by then, but the restaurant business was such a challenge to me that I immersed myself in it and blocked everything else out.

Weekends were particularly bad. "Do you have to go in to the restaurant?" Earle would furtively ask. "

Yeah, it's Saturday, the busiest night. They need all the help they can get," I would answer, detecting a bit of unhappiness in his voice.

But I was caught between my promise to Shizu, my desire to succeed, and my role of a wife who should be with my husband. I did not like to have to make this decision. But Earle never openly voiced his unhappiness about staying home alone on a Saturday, and I rationalized that this was a temporary situation and everything would return to normal when Shizu came back from Japan.

After two years, Earle and I were practically strangers. I knew we needed to get our marriage back on track and sought counseling from a family therapist.

"You guys need to have fun. You've got to indulge yourselves more!" the therapist told us.

I left the restaurant business to Mark and turned my attention to my marriage.

The summer of '85 was a time of reflection and renewal for Earle and me. I took up golf, Earle's passion but my disdain until that time.

We even revived our passion, ballroom dancing, which we had put in mothballs decades before. Earle bought me a beautiful, red lace dancing dress with fringes like in the flapper days, and I bought myself a pair of red dancing shoes. The fringes flipped around as we danced jitterbug at Moseley's on the Charles, one of a few ballrooms still operating in Boston. In the dimly lit ballroom under the glittering balls that hang from the ceiling, we danced our nights away to the sound of Johnnie Shea's Big Band. As we waltzed around and around the ballroom with the women in evening gowns, we were transported back forty years to our youths and realized how far we had drifted apart.

Ourselves Growing Older

Just as I was winding down my restaurant involvement, another adventure awaited me. In 1979, my article based on my survey on martial arts and women was published in a feminist newspaper, *The Equal Times.* Someone in the Boston Women's Health Book Collective read the article, liked it, and called me to ask if they could use my article in their next update of *Our Bodies Ourselves.*

"Of course," I said, "glad to be of help." I got my name in tiny print in the 1984 edition as one of the contributors.

"Contributers of Ourselves Growiing Older" c. 1987

OURSELVES, GROWING OLDER

By Paula Brown Doress and
Diana Laskin Siegal and
The Midlife and
Older Women Book Project

In cooperation with
The Boston Women's Health
Book Collective, authors of
The New Our Bodies, Ourselves

*WOMEN AGING WITH
KNOWLEDGE AND POWER*

In the fall of 1985, The Boston Women's Health Book Collective approached me about coming on board as one of the coauthors on their brand-new book, specially designed for older women. I was fifty-seven years old, had been through the ups and downs of marriage, had gone through an identity crisis, faced health challenges, raised three children, and was a grandmother. I thought I could bring something to the book for older women and accepted their invitation. There was no monetary reward, they told me. It didn't matter to me. The fact that I might be able to contribute, even in a minute way, to the betterment of older women's lives excited me.

Women of every shape, size, and background worked on the book, bringing their expertise or experiences to enrich it. The book dealt with every kind of challenge that older women face, from divorce to death of husband to cancer to financial difficulty. I helped with the section on what kind of healthy stress-coping methods were being utilized by older women. I interviewed several women and reported their stress-coping methods, ranging from having a pet to exercising. Under the able editorial leadership of Paula Doress Brown and Diana Segal, Simon and Schuster Company published *Ourselves Growing Older* in 1987, the first of such a book for older women

My Father's Legacy

In the spring of 1981, I met a Harvard professor who was researching on the history of Japanese management.

"Oh, my father pioneered in that field," I told him.

He asked me, "What is his name?"

"Toichiro Araki," I answered.

He looked stunned. "You are the daughter of Toichiro Araki?"

"Why?" I asked.

"He is in my thesis. In fact, I was hoping to go to Japan and meet him!"

"Oh, I'm so sorry," I told him. "My father died several years ago."

I felt the invisible hand of destiny again.

Dr. Andrew Gordon went to Japan and talked with my sisters and my father's colleagues who were still living. In 1987, he presented a paper on my father titled, "Araki Toichiro and the Shaping of Labor Management" at the International Conference on Business History in Japan, which was published in a book, *Japanese Management in Historical Perspective,* by Tokyo University Press, 1989.

A Japanese School!

The invisible hand of destiny with my American journey continued to guide me. I had finished writing for *Ourselves Growing Older* and was looking for work that would utilize my bicultural and bilingual skills.

One day, a heading in *The Boston Globe,* "A Japanese School Coming to Boston," jumped into my eyes. Showa Women's University in Tokyo was planning to open its study-abroad campus in Boston. "Internationalization" and "globalization" were the buzzwords of the 1980s. As my Japanese restaurant experience proved, Americans were expanding their gastronomic horizons far and wide and were fast becoming the sushi epicures of the western world.

The '60s and '70s "hippie" movement brought "Zen" and "satori" into the American vocabulary. The Japanese were coming to America for pleasure, study, or business in astounding numbers, and the Americans were turning their attention to the lucrative Japanese market.

I sent a letter and my résumé to the president of Showa Women's University in Tokyo, asking if I might be of help in opening their branch in Boston. Within a week, I received a call. "Yes, please come and join us. We need a bilingual and bicultural person who knows Boston!"

On April 3, 1988, the opening day of the school, I went to work as a cultural advisor for Showa Boston Institute for Language and Culture on Moss Hill in Jamaica Plain. To my surprise, I found that the parent school, Showa Women's University in Tokyo, was also a survivor of the war, losing its entire campus in the 1945 Tokyo bombings. Yet, Showa's president had decided to establish a branch in the United States, to give Japanese women a global view and to help bring peace to the world. I felt as if I had found my soul mate.

The horrific deaths and suffering of World War I produced many pacifists around the world. In 1920, Enkichi Hitomi, an idealistic poet and scholar, and Midori, his college-educated wife (a rarity in 1920s Japan), fervently wished for world peace and founded a school based on the philosophy of Leo Tolstoy and also of Henry David Thoreau, American essayist. The school's purpose was to educate women to help build a peaceful world. It began with only eight students on a shoestring operation in a rented room in Tokyo. This was the beginning of Showa Women's University.

Over the years, through blood, sweat, and tears of the founders and a few like-minded educators, the school grew to an educational system from high school through university, all on one campus in Tokyo. In the spring of 1945, the school was razed to ashes in the Tokyo fire-bombings. Teachers, staff, and students all made unbelievable sacrifices and labored tirelessly to clear the debris and to rebuild the school. Old photos show the founder and the president pushing a wheelbarrow piled with debris and teachers and students picking through the rubble.

They did not dwell on their sufferings and, looking to the future, began rebuilding the school. By 1951, they had added kindergarten and elementary schools. But in1955, the school was destroyed by fire. As if a phoenix rising again, Showa began to rebuild itself, this time with concrete buildings. Now they were a complete educational system from kindergarten to graduate school on a sprawling campus in Tokyo. Kusuo Hitomi, the founder's son, became the president. He, too, believed in women's power to help build a peaceful world.

The world had changed since the founding of the school. Countries around the world were becoming more interconnected. The younger Hitomi realized that, if Japanese women were to play a role in peace-building, they must shed their parochial island mentality and become more internationally minded, and to achieve this, they must leave Japan and experience a foreign culture. He decided to open a branch in America to send his students to meet people of different roots, ethnic backgrounds, and beliefs and to study English.

Cries of opposition rose from the parents: "You are not going to send my precious daughter to that gun-loving, violent country!"

He searched far and wide for an appropriate place and settled for Boston.

New England and Boston have a long history with Japan. The first American to visit Edo (Tokyo) in 1853 was a New Englander, Commodore Perry. Boston and Kyoto, the ancient capital of Japan, are sister cities. Many renowned Japan scholars are at Harvard University. Boston's Museum of Fine Arts has the largest Japanese collection in the world, outside of Japan. Kusuo Hitomi felt it was appropriate that his students come to Boston, a city so rich in American history and with strong ties with Japan. He assured the parents that every precaution would be taken to keep students safe.

No Japanese school had ever opened a branch in America. Showa was the pioneer. There was no one to guide us how to proceed. We were all amateurs in a sense. We were feeling our way, setting precedents, making mistakes, and getting back on track again. After the first few years of struggle, we wondered if we could really make a go of it, but we persevered, Japanese and American administrators and teachers working together as a team.

I became the director of student life, and was a surrogate mother to two hundred young women from Japan, many of whom had never left their country or parents. Adjustments in climate, food, language, lifestyle, and customs were enormous. This was a residential school, and roommate problems, homesickness, or just plain nervousness about being in a foreign country created a tense environment, which we tried to diffuse. The students' safety was first and foremost. I knew that the Japanese girls were not brought up to be as independent as American girls and lacked street savvy. The first year we were all so nervous about any incident that we had a curfew of 5:30 p.m., and the students had to go out in threes!

All the experience of my early years in America came in handy, helping me to understand and give support and guidance to the students. I knew their fears and anxieties, although the Showa Boston environment was far more stable and welcoming than the one I'd first encountered in Illinois forty years before.

Building the Bridge

I devoted twenty years to the institute as a mentor and surrogate mother, giving cultural and life guidance to over six thousand young Japanese women who came to Showa Boston to study English and American culture. More than anything else, what these women gained was a sense of self and a broader view on life. My days were long and often included weekends and nights. Sometimes I would wake in cold sweat having a bad dream about my students.

Earle, now retired, volunteered for the supper preparation duty. Every night when I dragged myself home exhausted, he would have a hot meal ready for us. He even accompanied me and a student to the emergency room in the nearby hospital when the student became ill in the middle of the night. I was never so glad to have Earle near me on such nights. I know that without his full support I could never have given the kind of time and energy I gave to my students. He was my helpmate in the truest sense.

Showa Women's University and I, both survivors of Tokyo bombings, found a common ground together, to build a bridge of peace between Japan and America.

EPILOGUE:

END OF THE JOURNEY

An invisible hand of destiny planted the seed of my American journey in a musty attic in Tokyo in the 1930s when I was a child. It led me to the old steamer trunk that crossed the ocean with my father, where I "met" smiling Americans in the old, yellowed photos that depicted my father's student days in Akron, Ohio, in 1920. An idea rose in my little heart: *I want to meet these friendly smiling people called Americans!* That seed led me to study English in college. Even when the two nations were at war, and even when the bombs fell upon us, and even in the darkest hours, I held on to that dream. I never dreamt that my beloved country would fall and be occupied by Americans!

But an invisible hand of destiny brought my husband to me. Out of billions of people in the world, why him? The Pacific War was not in my equation; nor were the horrific bombings of my beloved city. Not all Americans were happy or friendly. America was not a land of sugar and honey. But it is a land of possibilities that we create.

There were many unexpected hindrances along the way. I fell down so many times, and I almost gave up, but somehow I picked myself up and continued. The invisible hand led me from one unexpected challenge to another. Now, I'm almost at the end of my long journey. I don't know what the invisible hand of destiny that guided me for eighty-two years has in store for me, but each day when I wake up, I open the window, look up at the sky and say, "Thank you."

Made in the USA
Lexington, KY
28 April 2016